# THE LOVE OF MOUNTAINS

Michael Crawford Poole

# THE LOVE
# OF MOUNTAINS

CRESCENT BOOKS
New York

# CONTENTS

**First published in Great Britain in 1980
by Octopus Books Limited,
59 Grosvenor Street, London W1.**

This edition published by Crescent Books

© Octopus Books Limited, MCMLXXX

Library of Congress Cataloging in Publication Data
   Poole, Michael, 1946-
      Love of mountains.
      1. Mountains.  I. Title.
GB511.P66      500.9'14'3      79-18269

ISBN 0 517 29625 X

Produced by Mandarin Publishers Limited
22a Westlands Road, Quarry Bay, Hong Kong.

Printed in Hong Kong

# FOREWORD

## by Chris Bonington

Endpapers: aerial view of Cape Town and Table Mountain, South Africa.

Page 1: Nordend, 4,609 m (15,122 ft), is one of the ten Monte Rosa peaks that divide Switzerland from Italy, and central from southern Europe.

Pages 2–3: dawn on the East Ridge of Mount Cook and a fine view of New Zealand's Southern Alps. The 3,764 m (12,349 ft) peak towers some 2,400 m (8,000 ft) above its glaciers.

Page 4: Monarch of the Rockies, Mt Robson, 3,954 m (12,972 ft), fills the sky as it is viewed here from Mt Resplendent.

Left: the stupendous North-West Face of Half Dome in the Yosemite National Park. In 1865 the California Geological Survey stated that: '. . . Half Dome is a crest of granite rising to a height of 4,737 ft (1,444 m) above the valley, perfectly inaccessible, and probably the only one of all the prominent points about the Yosemite which never has been, and never will be, trodden by human foot . . .' Today there are at least four major routes on the North-West Face alone.

A love of mountains is an addictive passion from which you will never want to escape. My own love started when I was sixteen; I was captivated by a book of pictures of the Scottish hills and imagined myself scrambling over the monochrome ridges of the Cuillins of Skye and across the rolling whalebacks of the Mamores and the Trossachs. Fantasy became reality later on that summer when I stayed with my grandfather who lived just outside Dublin. I ventured into the Wicklow Hills and experienced as great a sense of adventure as I was to discover in later years on my first visit to the Alps or even the giant Himalaya.

In building a life around the mountains one becomes part of an evolving sport; the equipment one uses, the rules or ethics one observes, the climbs one chooses or even pioneers, are all part of the greater framework determined by one's predecessors.

All of us who were lucky enough to go to the South West Face of Everest in the autumn of 1975 were intensely conscious of the landmarks delineated by our forerunners and the part that they had played, and we were about to play, in the story of this magnificent mountain.

This book captures the beauty and grandeur of the world's mountains in its magnificent pictures and, at the same time, outlines the rich history of man's effort to climb them.

# WORLD MAP OF MOUNTAINS

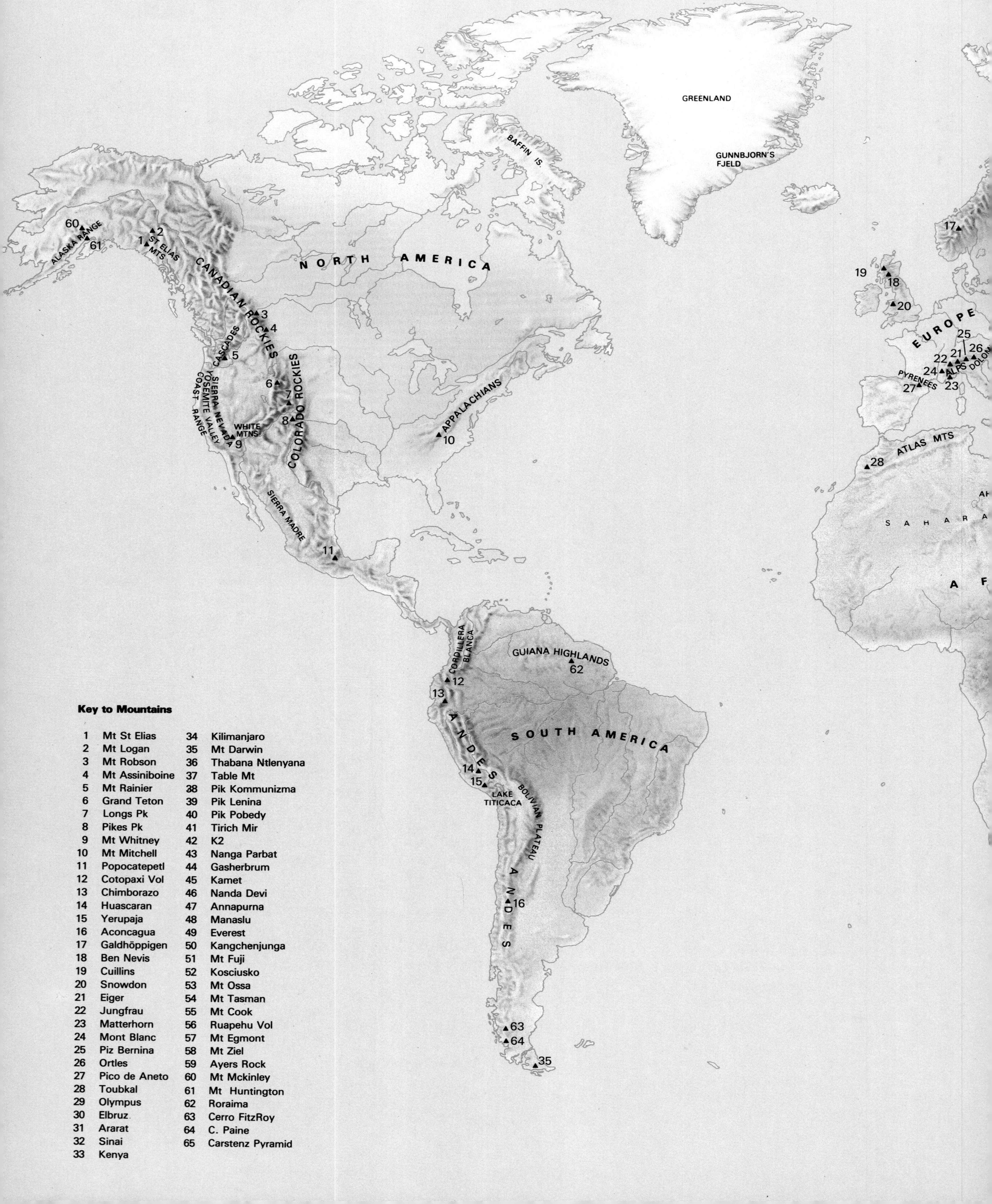

GREENLAND

BAFFIN IS.

GUNNBJORN'S FJELD

NORTH AMERICA

ALASKA RANGE

60
61
1
2 St ELIAS MTS

CANADIAN ROCKIES

3
4
CASCADES
5
SIERRA NEVADA
COAST RANGE
YOSEMITE VALLEY
6
7
COLORADO ROCKIES
8
WHITE MTNS
9

10 APPALACHIANS

SIERRA MADRE

11

17

19
18
20

EUROPE
25
22 21 26 DOLOM
24 ALPS 23
PYRENEES
27

ATLAS MTS
28

SAHARA

AF

CORDILLERA BLANCA
12
13
GUIANA HIGHLANDS
62

SOUTH AMERICA

ANDES

14
15
LAKE TITICACA
BOLIVIAN PLATEAU

ANDES

16

63
64
35

**Key to Mountains**

| | | | |
|---|---|---|---|
| 1 | Mt St Elias | 34 | Kilimanjaro |
| 2 | Mt Logan | 35 | Mt Darwin |
| 3 | Mt Robson | 36 | Thabana Ntlenyana |
| 4 | Mt Assiniboine | 37 | Table Mt |
| 5 | Mt Rainier | 38 | Pik Kommunizma |
| 6 | Grand Teton | 39 | Pik Lenina |
| 7 | Longs Pk | 40 | Pik Pobedy |
| 8 | Pikes Pk | 41 | Tirich Mir |
| 9 | Mt Whitney | 42 | K2 |
| 10 | Mt Mitchell | 43 | Nanga Parbat |
| 11 | Popocatepetl | 44 | Gasherbrum |
| 12 | Cotopaxi Vol | 45 | Kamet |
| 13 | Chimborazo | 46 | Nanda Devi |
| 14 | Huascaran | 47 | Annapurna |
| 15 | Yerupaja | 48 | Manaslu |
| 16 | Aconcagua | 49 | Everest |
| 17 | Galdhöppigen | 50 | Kangchenjunga |
| 18 | Ben Nevis | 51 | Mt Fuji |
| 19 | Cuillins | 52 | Kosciusko |
| 20 | Snowdon | 53 | Mt Ossa |
| 21 | Eiger | 54 | Mt Tasman |
| 22 | Jungfrau | 55 | Mt Cook |
| 23 | Matterhorn | 56 | Ruapehu Vol |
| 24 | Mont Blanc | 57 | Mt Egmont |
| 25 | Piz Bernina | 58 | Mt Ziel |
| 26 | Ortles | 59 | Ayers Rock |
| 27 | Pico de Aneto | 60 | Mt Mckinley |
| 28 | Toubkal | 61 | Mt Huntington |
| 29 | Olympus | 62 | Roraima |
| 30 | Elbruz | 63 | Cerro FitzRoy |
| 31 | Ararat | 64 | C. Paine |
| 32 | Sinai | 65 | Carstenz Pyramid |
| 33 | Kenya | | |

S O V I E T    U N I O N

U R A L S

A S I A

CARPATHIANS

29

CAUCASUS
30
31

TIEN SHAN

38  PAMIRS
40    39

HINDU KUSH KARAKORUM
41  43  45  44
42
GARWHAL  RANGE
46
47 48
H I M A L A Y A S
49  NEPAL
50

TIBET

CHINA

JAPAN
JAPANESE
ALPS
51

32

ESTI
S

I C A

ETHIOPIAN
HIGHLANDS

RUWENZORI MTS

33
34

INDIA

36
DRAKENSBERG

HEXRIVIERBERGE

65  NEW
GUINEA

AUSTRALIA
58
MACDONNELL
RANGES
59
MUSGRAVE
RANGE

GREAT DIVIDING RANGE

52
SNOWY MTS
AUSTRALIAN
ALPS

NEW  57
ZEALAND
56
55
54
SOUTHERN
ALPS

53

TASMANIA

# EUROPE

Only in the past two hundred years have the mystery and terror long linked with the world's greatest mountains been dissipated. From the beginning of recorded history until the 18th century the summits remained inviolate. People did not climb for sport, and the idea of loving mountains was completely foreign. Most western peoples regarded mountains with abhorrence. They seemed too chaotic and wild to those who sought an orderly, civilized world. In the East, however, attitudes were different. There, mountains were religiously revered and appreciated for their aesthetic qualities. Yet few were ever climbed, and then never just for fun.

Suddenly, in a mere two hundred years, every major peak in the world has been 'conquered'. Climbers of many different nations, men and women from all walks of life, enjoy spending time and money in meeting the challenge of tackling rock and ice faces. Some write books and sell films about their exploits; commercial interests and governments alike are keen to sponsor them. Each year some 30 million skiers take to the slopes for fun. What has brought about this relatively rapid change in our view of the mountains? How is it that so many now find both spiritual and physical recreation where so few found it before?

The answer lies in an essentially European development, the product of new ideas that in two turbulent centuries have totally altered our control of the natural world, and the way we see it.

The first change in ideas was the breaking down of the age-old fear of angering the Gods by examining the natural world too closely. This freed men's minds for science. The second major change in ideas was the reaction against pure, absolutist reason sparked off by the philosopher Jean-Jacques Rousseau (1712–1778), which produced European Romanticism.

If it seems strange to talk in terms of philosophy about such practical matters as rock climbing, or skiing, or simply enjoying a fine view and fresh mountain air, it is nonetheless true that, without the revolution in attitudes towards the natural world that came about in Europe in the 18th century, the great ranges of the world might well have remained unexplored and unclimbed, as they had done since the dawn of history.

These changes have freed us to love mountains, each in our own way. It is a love that is part active, part contemplative, and which has developed to embrace the farthest corners of the world. By unshackling their minds from superstition and fear, people have discovered one of the best environments in which to seek out the limits of human experience, both spiritual and physical.

## The Alps

These famous mountains stretch in a great crescent from the Maritime Alps just north of Nice on the Mediterranean, up to the Central Alps and Mont Blanc, the highest of them all, and then sweep eastwards, forming the frontiers of France, Germany, Switzerland, Italy, Austria and Yugoslavia; and with a small break they continue east in another great arc as the Carpathians.

People have lived among these mountains for hundreds of generations, but they hardly ventured above the snow line, and if they did, they did not climb very high or stay long. By and large the mountains remained obstacles to be got round or through; they were seen as threatening, and few people could see that any pleasure was to be had from them.

'I have been on the Mount of Jove,' wrote Master John de Bremble, a monk of Christ Church, Canterbury, after crossing the St Bernard Pass in 1188, 'on the one hand looking up to the heavens of the mountains, on the other, shuddering at the hell of the valleys, feeling myself so much nearer heaven that I was sure that my prayer would be heard. "Lord," I said, "restore me to my brethren, that I may tell them that they come not to this place of torment." Place of torment indeed, where the marble pavement of the stony ground is ice alone, and you cannot set your foot safely; where, strange to say, although it is so slippery that you cannot stand, the death into which there is every facility for a fall is certain death.'

Not all men of earlier times shared

Pages 10–11: the Italian Dolomites boast climbing and scenery to rival the best in the world. Here the church of St Maddalena nestles in a lush valley below the jagged peak of Fermedaturme in the Geislergruppe of the western Dolomites. Today the Dolomites are Italian territory, but it was not always so. Until the First World War much of this mountain domain was in Austrian hands under the Hapsburg Emperors and some of the towns still echo such past glories. Even today much of the population is still German speaking.

It is a lovely area with impossible fairy-tale spires and rock walls of grey, brown and yellow forming a backdrop to flower-covered meadows, orchards and hayfields: but the scars of bitter wartime fighting are still to be found among the crags, with fortifications hewn from the living rock and tangles of rusting wire. The wealth of ice- and rock-climbing is breathtaking and has influenced the development of climbing throughout Europe.

Left: the beautiful Mont Blanc range in the French Alps which, for the climber, are the most interesting and exciting group in the European Alps. The central snow dome of the massif is flanked by a host of jagged peaks which together hold more than 2,000 climbs, among them some of the best and most famous routes in the world. To the left is the north face of the 3,900 m (12,795 ft) Aiguille d'Argentière, first climbed in 1864 by Whymper during the Golden Age of mountaineering, when the main peaks of Europe were climbed for the first time.

Master John's antipathy for mountain scenery or were so fearful. In 350 BC Philip of Macedon climbed Mount Haemus in the Balkans, hoping to see both the Aegean and Adriatic seas from its summit, while in 1335 AD Petrarch climbed the 1,960 m (6,430 ft) Mont Ventoux. In the 13th century Peter III of Aragon climbed Pic Canigou, 2,784 m (9,135 ft) high, in the Pyrenees 'to ascertain what there was on the top of it.' He found a lake and 'when he threw a stone into the lake, a horrible dragon of enormous size came out of it, and began to fly about in the air, and to darken the air with its breath', wrote his chronicler.

The first properly recorded rock climb in Europe was that of Antoine de Ville, Lord of Dompjulien and Beaupré who as *capitaine des schelliers* to King Charles VIII was in command of men trained to scale the walls of besieged castles and cities. In 1492 he climbed the near vertical walls of Mont Aiguille in Southern France, a 2,096 m (6,880 ft) bastion popularly known as 'Mont Inaccessible'. As one member of his party wrote, they 'had to ascend half a league by ladders and then a league by a route horrible to behold and even more terrible to come down than to go up'. It was an exploit that required all the skill and technical expertise of the day.

This was essentially a military exercise, but other early mountaineers such as the Zurich naturalist Conrad Gesner climbed for quite different reasons.

'I have resolved for the future,' he wrote to a friend in 1541, 'so long as God grants me life, to ascend divers mountains every year, or at least one, in the season when vegetation is at its height, partly for botanical observation, partly for the worthy exercise of the body and recreation of the mind. What must be the pleasure, think you, what the delight of a mind rightly touched, to gaze upon the huge mountain masses for one's show, and, as it were, lift one's head into the clouds. The soul is strangely rapt with these astonishing heights, and carried off to the contemplation of the one supreme Architect. Philosophers will always feast the eye of body and mind on the goodly things of this earthly paradise; and by no means least among these are the abruptly soaring summits, the trackless steeps, the vast slopes rising to the sky, the rugged rocks, the shady woods.'

Here for the first time are set out the three chief motives for climbing which were to power the first era of mountain

exploration: these were the need to satisfy scientific curiosity, and the need for achieving the 'worthy exercise of the body and recreation of the mind.'

Gesner started no movement – that was not to come until the 18th century – but when we consider his words on the contemplation of the supreme Architect it is not so surprising that the first mountaineers were clerics, the 'muscular Christians' as they have been called. In 1779 the prior of the hospice of the Great St Bernard, Monsignor Murith, climbed Mont Velan. At 3,765 m (12,353 ft), it was then the highest summit in the Alps to have been climbed. In 1784, Curé Clément of Champéry climbed the highest peak of the Dents du Midi, while in 1788 Father Placidus à Spesecha reached the top of Stockgren in the Tödi range of Switzerland. This was the first of a long series of ascents in his exploration

Left: the magnificent south face of Mont Blanc and the frontier ridge of Mont Mondit from the Italian side. This mighty 3,350 m (11,000 ft) face of ice and granite is of Himalayan grandeur and has drawn climbers to it in both summer and winter.

Mont Blanc is the highest summit in Western Europe, at 4,807 m (15,771 ft), and its ascent in 1786 by Dr Paccard and Jacques Balmat marked the beginning of modern mountaineering, freeing men of the old superstition that the gods would be angered and that it would be fatal to spend a night out above the snow line. Perhaps because its lovely snow-capped summit can be seen from Geneva, Mont Blanc was the first major peak to be attempted. Within a few years of its conquest, a steady stream of adventurous tourists was being guided to the top – but not by this face – and the sport of climbing spread from there.

Today a 9·5 km (6 mile) tunnel under the mountain links the Italian centre of Courmayeur with Chamonix, which is now the most important ski and climbing resort in France.

Above right: this beautiful bird, the lammergeyer vulture, was almost extinct in Europe, but is now slowly increasing in number. It is found almost exclusively in wild mountain areas and is usually seen soaring alone. With its narrow 2·7 m (109 in) wingspan it is easily distinguished from the smaller eagles, buzzards and kites.

Right: edelweiss, the inspiration of song and poem, has become almost synonymous with high mountain places. It grows above the timber line to beyond 3,100 m (10,100 ft) in the Alps.

of the Tödi, culminating in 1824, when he was 72, in an attempt on the Tödi itself. He climbed to within 275 metres (900 ft) of the summit and, though exhausted himself, he had the satisfaction of seeing his two chamois-hunter companions reach the top.

Although à Spesecha had little influence outside his own area of the Glarner Alps, he lived to see the beginning of popular mountaineering in the Chamonix valley. By the time he died, the highest peak in the Alps, Mont Blanc, had become a new item on the 'Grand Tour' of young gentlefolk 'doing' Europe.

## Mont Blanc

In 1760 a Genevese naturalist, Horace-Bénédict de Saussure, visited Chamonix and was enchanted with the unspoiled valley. He reconnoitered some

of the surrounding heights and offered a prize to the first person who could find a route to the top of Mont Blanc. It was not until some 15 years later that any serious effort was made, but meanwhile interest in mountains gathered pace. Naturalists, physicians and geologists visited the Alps. The origin and distribution of glaciers fascinated them, as did the study of man's physical limitations. Local men experienced in mountain travel began to act as professional guides, and some of the lower peaks were climbed successfully.

In June 1786 a 25-year-old local man, Jacques Balmat, made an attempt to claim Saussure's prize. He knew the lower slopes of Mont Blanc quite well, having searched there for crystals and hunted chamois. He pressed on up the mountain until it grew dark, when he sheltered in a crevasse for the night. The next day he returned to Chamonix with his face badly burned by snow glare, but he had dispelled the ancient superstition that it was fatal to spend a night above the snow line. He took his peeling face to the local doctor, Michel-Gabriel Paccard, who was himself interested in making scientific observations from the summit of Europe's highest peak. They joined forces and set out on 8 August. They were lucky with the weather, for they were dressed as for a valley walk and carried only an alpenstock each, a long wooden pole tipped with an iron ferrule. By the next afternoon they were approaching the summit.

'As I rose higher,' Balmat wrote later, 'the air became much less easy to breathe, and I had to stop almost every ten steps and wheeze like one with consumption. I felt as if my lungs had gone and my chest was quite empty ... The cold got worse and worse, and to go a quarter of a

league took an hour.' They slogged on, watching the snow at their feet. Suddenly they were there. 'I looked round, trembling for fear that there might be some further new unattainable aiguille. But no! no! I no longer had any strength to go higher; the muscles of my legs seemed only held together by my trousers. But behold I was at the end of my journey; I was on a spot where no living being had ever been before, no eagle nor even a chamois! I was the monarch of Mont Blanc! I was the statue on this unique pedestal.'

Paccard, who got little credit for his efforts for the next hundred years, thanks to Balmat characterizing him as a millstone around his own neck, proceeded to make scientific observations for the next half hour. They were 4,807 metres (15,771 ft) high on the top

Top left: the chances of coming as close as this to a Golden Eagle, on her nest with a chick, are pretty remote. Although it is the most common eagle in Europe, its numbers are declining and it is found only in the wildest mountain areas.
Centre left: the orange lily – *Lilium croceum* – is one of the most beautiful wild flowers that grow in the lush hay meadows of the Dolomites.
Below left: two male Ibex fight over a mate in the spring, the clash of their horns echoing among the mountain crags. Ibex are wild goats and there are several species in the mountains of Europe, Asia and Africa. The male has large, curved, strongly ridged horns.

Right: a climber picks his way across the ice-bound north face of the Doldenhorn, 3,643 m (11,952 ft), in the Bernese Oberland. This is the last peak of the Blümlisalp chain that rises above Kandersteg, a part of the north face of the European Alps overlooking the plains of north-west Europe. The top of the 701 m (2,300 ft) high face is guarded by a tricky band of steep and crumbly limestone, while on the skyline is the North East Ridge, a classic ice-arête.
  Notice how the rope is led through a running belay or 'runner' consisting of an ice piton set in the face, to which is attached a nylon tape sling and a karabiner with a spring-loaded gate. The rope is led through the 'Krab' and if the lead man falls he will only travel the length of the rope between himself and the runner before being held by his companion – instead of falling the full length of the rope. He is using these aids as 'protection' rather than to assist his climb with them. This is classic ice climbing with the leader balanced on the front points of his crampons and using the sharp spikes of his ice-axe and peg hammer instead of finding or cutting hand- and foot-holds.

of Europe, with the magnificent view of the Alps to admire, 'its four hundred glaciers shining in the sunlight'.

However, this wonderful experience was short-lived; they were back in Chamonix the following day with frost-bitten fingers, and almost blinded by snow glare. Undaunted by such hazards, de Saussure himself was successful the following year.

These ascents ushered in the era of climbing that has continued unabated to this day. The old superstitions had been shown to be groundless. Men could breathe at height, and they could even survive a night on the mountains. No spirits, demons, or Gods had been unduly angered. Gradually, the scientific excuse for climbing mountains gave way to climbing just for the fun of it. Mountains became tourist attractions. In 1809 the first woman reached the summit of Mont Blanc. She was an 18-year-old local peasant girl, Maria Paradis. The ascent by Henriette d'Angeville 29 years later was for a long while referred to as the first ascent by a woman. Indeed, in the late 19th century the competition among the women became quite as intense as that among the men, particularly between the Americans and the British. Women proved themselves very competent mountaineers, despite the problems of conventional dress.

## Other Mountain Sports

Climbing was not the only mountain activity that was beginning to become popular. The first winter sports holiday was held at the Kulm Hotel, St Moritz, in 1865 and it was largely devoted to tobogganing, skating and sleigh riding. Skiing was first introduced to Switzerland in 1868. In the same year a nearly illiterate Norwegian cottager, Sondre Ouersen Norheim, travelled from Morgedal in Telemark to Oslo and displayed to an amazed public the first modern controlled skiing. He had invented or developed a waisted, arched ski to which the heels and toes were firmly held; this became known as the 'Telemark ski'. It was the beginning of a sport which now has some 30 million participants each year, worldwide.

Skiing itself is of unknown antiquity. Skis dating back to 2,500 BC have been found in the Altai Mountains of Khazakstan in central Asia, and at Hoting in Sweden. The earliest known writings on skiing are in Chinese, with a 7th-century account of the Kirgiz (Turkish) tribe 'who skim over the ice on wooden horses (MuMa) which they bind to their feet'. Skiing had been a part of daily life in Scandinavia from prehistoric times and it was Scandinavian migrants to North America and Australia who brought skiing to those countries, where it caught on as a sport slightly earlier than it did in Europe. The first ski club in the world was founded at Kiandra, Australia, in 1861. The opening of the first club in America followed in 1867 at La Porte, California.

Nansen's crossing of the Greenland ice cap on Telemark skis in 1888 brought skiing to the notice of the general public. Soon afterwards Matthias Zdarsky, an Austrian reserve officer, developed a new technique of skiing on the rough terrain of the Alps, and started his school at Lilienfeld near Vienna in 1896. The type of skiing that Zdarsky developed, enabling the skier to turn, brake, and control high speeds over steep and broken ground, also required the development of specialized equipment. Within a short time this new Alpine skiing equipment became incompatible with the more traditional Nordic style of skiing, which concentrated on touring.

Alpine skiing has itself developed over the years into several disciplines, both competitive and recreational. The competitive area has concentrated on the downhill, the slalom and the flying kilometre, while the recreational side has produced ski-mountaineering and high-level touring through ranges such as the Alps. Also, in recent years there have appeared specialized acrobatics known as aerials, and also ski ballet. Both these new disciplines are still in a state of rapid development, and are part recreational and part competitive. Through them shorter skis have become more popular.

The enormous boom in skiing in this century has been brought about partly by the increase in the amount of time and money people have to spend, and partly by the mechanization of mountain areas with lifts and chairs and railways that take most of the effort out of getting to the top of the slopes.

Other mountain sports that have become popular are bobsleighing, hang gliding and various combinations of skiing, hang gliding and parachuting.

## The Golden Age

The so-called Golden Age of climbing in Europe began with the ascent of the Wetterhorn in 1854 by the Englishman Alfred Wills, and ended in 1865 with the triumph of another Englishman, Edward Whymper, on the Matterhorn, and the disaster on the descent in which four of his party were killed.

During this eleven-year period many

Left: Mont Ponset, 2,825 m (9,268 ft), *right* and Cayre de la Madone *centre*, viewed from the south-west. The upper left skyline of Ponset is the long west ridge, famous for its classic rock-climb routes. This part of the *Alpes Maritimes* is only some 50 km (31 miles) from the Mediterranean, and both climate and flora in the valley bottoms are sub-tropical.

of Europe's most beautiful and difficult peaks were climbed for the first time. More than 60 peaks in all were conquered, notably Monte Rosa above Zermatt, the Eiger, the Pelmo in the Dolomites, and the Aiguille Verte in the Mont Blanc range.

Most of these achievements were British, although during the previous 30 years the Swiss, the Germans and the French had made numerous first ascents. The remarkable thing about the Golden Age was that some 31 out of the 39 really important climbs were made by the British, according to the American mountaineer and historian W. A. B. Coolidge, who himself climbed the last great rock peak of the Alps, the Meije, with his aunt, Miss Meta Brevoort. The standards and prejudices of these people set the tone for all European climbing at a formative period, and became so predominant as to create the

Top right: the beautiful Sciora Cirque in the Bregaglia Alps which form the frontier of Italy and Switzerland. Here they are seen from the north-west; *left to right*, the peaks are Fuori, Pioda, Ago and Dentro, with the Bondasca Glacier tumbling down on the extreme right. These unlikely looking towers of rough grey granite hold excellent routes for all grades of climbing, some of them up to 550 m (1,800 ft) in length.

Right: sea-cliff climbing at its best on the splendid granite face of Great Zawn at Bosigran in Cornwall. The climber, Pete Livesy, is negotiating a tricky part of the route known as 'Dream' high above the crashing of the Atlantic waves. Sea-cliff climbing has a history stretching back to medieval times, when men scrambled down knotted ropes to take birds' eggs. Towards the end of the last century British mountaineers began to use the home cliffs as practice grounds for their Alpine adventures and found them 'quite sensational'. However, it was not until the 1960s that sea-cliff climbing really caught on in Britain.

Left: a skier executes a spectacular back flip in a demonstration of aerial skiing. Aerials are one of the three disciplines used for the World Freestyle Championships, the others being ski-ballet and Moguls, otherwise known as 'the bumps'. Ski-ballet is somewhat akin to figure-skating on skis to music, and includes a fair amount of gymnastics. Freestyle skiing originated in America during the 1960s. You need to be a very expert skier before beginning this sport.

illusion that climbing was a British sport. The climbers were mostly in the professions, clergymen, or men of independent means.

Technique was still primitive. The climbers carried ropes but had little idea how to use them properly. The ice axe was almost unknown and the alpenstock had hardly changed since Saussure's time. Steps were often cut in the ice with a hatchet.

The Alpine Club was formed in London in 1857 and was almost exclusively for serious British climbers. Other clubs were soon formed in Europe and, while they attracted many fine climbers, they tended to have as many mountain lovers as mountaineers. More and more people were taking to the mountains for recreation and this development was hastened by the extension of railways into mountain areas.

As early as the 1860s the Matterhorn was regarded as 'the last great problem of the Alps' – the first of many peaks, crags and faces to bear this challenging title. Many believed it could not be climbed. 'There seemed to be a cordon drawn round it, up to which one might go, but no further', Edward Whymper wrote. 'The superstitious natives ... warned one against rash approach, lest the infuriate demons from their impregnable heights might hurl down vengeance for one's derision.'

Whymper made eight attempts on the Matterhorn before he was finally successful in 1865; but his success was immediately followed by probably the most infamous of Alpine disasters. 'Whymper did not dream of the ascent: he desired it – and he was impatient', wrote Gaston Rebuffat, who himself climbed the mountain as a guide and wrote a book devoted to it.

Whymper and his party set out on a cloudless morning, on 13 July 1865, to try the Swiss Ridge. They soon found that its seemingly impregnable steepness had been an optical illusion. Places that looked unclimbable from below 'were so easy that we could run about', Whymper wrote later.

The view that Whymper's party enjoyed from the summit (which they reached the next day) was stupendous. To the west the summit of Mont Blanc glowed in the sunlight, and they could see the Maritime Alps 209 km (130 miles) away to the south, as well as the Bernese Oberland away to the north across the Rhône valley.

'We remained on the summit for one hour –
"One crowded hour of glorious life."
'It passed away too quickly, and we began to prepare for the descent.'

On the descent four of the party fell, roped together. Whymper and his guide, 'Old' Peter Taugwalder, clung to the rocks. The rope tautened with a sharp jerk.

'We held; but the rope broke midway between Taugwalder and Lord Francis Douglas. For a few seconds we saw our unfortunate companions sliding downwards on their backs, spreading out their hands, endeavouring to save themselves. They passed from our sight uninjured, disappeared one by one, and fell from precipice to precipice on to the Matterhorn Glacier below, a distance of nearly 4,000 ft (1,219 m) in height.'

Whymper wrote later, 'Others may tread its summit-snows, but none will ever know the feelings of those who first gazed upon its marvellous panorama; and none, I trust, will ever be compelled to tell of joy turned to grief, and of laughter into mourning ... a momentary negligence may destroy the happiness of a lifetime.'

The accident created a public outcry against mountaineering and held up development for a generation. Then, gradually, the pace quickened again. New 'last great problems' were found to entice the climber to the more difficult crags and faces of mountains that had already been climbed. From these evolved rock-climbing as a separate sport.

## Britain

In Britain, the climbers who achieved so much in the Alps also discovered the attractions of Wales, the Peaks, the Lake District and Scotland as practice grounds. But these 19th-century pioneers were very different from the thousands of climbers who visit these areas today. The finest climber of the age, George Mallory, who was later killed on Everest (in 1924), wrote:

'Climbing for them means something more than common amusement ... A day well spent in the Alps is like some great symphony ... The spirit goes on a journey just as does the body ... The individual is in a sense submerged, yet not so as to be less conscious; rather his consciousness is specially alert, and he comes to a finer realization of himself than ever

Ben Nevis, at 1,343 m (4,406 ft), is the highest mountain in Britain. Its huge North East Face is seen here up the valley of Allt a'Mhuilinn from across the Caledonian Canal in the Great Glen. The great wall on the right-hand side of the valley is the largest crag in Britain, 3 km (2 miles) long and some 610 m (2,000 ft) high in places. It provides some of the most demanding routes in the country, although of course the summit can be reached by an easy hill walk. The picture was taken in June and good snow conditions are frequently experienced even in May. Some snow remains at the summit throughout most summers, particularly in north-facing gullies.

before. It is these moments of supremely harmonious experience that remain always with us and part of us.'

Another great climber, Geoffrey Winthrop Young, wrote of this period:

'The name of the game was rock climbing and they were all devoted to it. But there was more to it than that. They respected courage and skill on the crags but the most important thing to them was the spirit in which a man climbed. They sought not just the companionship of the rope but social companionship in the evenings and the intellectual exhilaration that comes from encountering keen and clear-minded argument ... Fundamentally, the route they were seeking was one that would take them closer to their own souls.'

It was much the same idea that the poet Samuel Taylor Coleridge had captured a hundred years earlier: 'The farther I ascend from animated Nature, from men, and cattle, and the common birds of the woods and fields, the greater becomes in me the Intensity of the feeling of Life.'

Now that the day has come when a climber must rack his brains to find something unclimbed to attempt anywhere in Europe, it is worth recalling the feelings of those who had this pleasure and the words to express it. Here is Geoffrey Young again, after a 'first' climb he made on a Welsh crag:

'... and I thrilled suddenly with a new feeling. For hundreds and thousands of years, high and close above the passing and repassing of countless generations, this upright corner of beautiful and solid England – or rather Wales – had been waiting unvisited, untrodden, even unseen, until, during a few days of my own short life, the climbing enthusiasm had broken over us, and had set me, miraculously, upon it. Here upon this ledge since earth took form out of chaos no one before me had set foot. On that glister of crystal quartz under my hand no eye before mine had ever rested. I tingled as I stood, to the very bootnails. And an enchantment as secret and enthralling as first love seemed opening behind and within all the unvisited cliffs and mountain walls in my sight.'

Technique was improving. The principles of rope work were being established, though not always accepted. Balance climbing rather than brute force became the fashion, while the alpenstock and the hatchet were combined to give the ice axe, which could be used with one hand. Hammers and pitons appeared, together with pebble chocks that could be inserted into a crack and the rope run behind to protect

Above: the savage North Face of the Eiger in the Bernese Alps, the scene of so much tragedy and triumph played out under the gaze of the world. Even in summer, as here, the Eiger's sunless North Face is plastered with snow and ice. Its grim, concave 1,402 m (4,600 ft) limestone face is called the 'Eigerwand' and sometimes dubbed the 'Mortwand' in memory of the many climbers who have lost their lives on it. After the tragedy of 1936 when four men died on the face (the last of them within reach of the rescuers who had climbed out through an embrasure of the remarkable Jungfrau railway that winds up inside the mountain), the Swiss authorities put the face out of bounds. This naturally increased its attraction to some climbers and ensured that tourists flocked to watch from below (the face is within sight of the hotels of Grindelwald). Colonel Strutt, editor of *The Alpine Journal*, wrote: 'The Eigerwand – still unscaled – continues to be an obsession for the mentally deranged of almost every nation. He who first succeeds may rest assured that he has accomplished the most imbecile variant since mountaineering first began.' Within six months, in July 1938, it was

accomplished by an Austro-German party. Long afterwards one of the victors, Heinrich Harrer, wrote: 'It has been widely deplored that the very creed of mountaineering should have been debased by climbs and attempts on this particular face, in that it has become an arena, a natural stage, on which every movement of the actors can be followed... Nobody regrets it more than the men themselves who climb on the Eiger's North Face. They desire nothing more than peace and quiet; they do not want to be looked at. They long for the days of their grandfathers when nobody took any notice of climbers or bothered to watch them.'

Since that 1938 epic the face has been climbed many times, in winter, solo, by women as well as men. There are now a number of routes including two 'direct' or straight-up routes.

Right: summer in the Swiss Pennine Alps. Three climbers pause to admire the view from the lower summit of the Rimpfischhorn, 4,199 m (13,777 ft).

the leader if he fell. The 'ethics' of such aids were hotly discussed.

After the First World War a more competitive way of climbing took over and the poetic, soul-seeking approach became submerged in nationalism. But still experience accumulated, each generation of mountaineers building on the experience of its predecessors.

## Conquest of the Eiger

Nationalistic competitiveness drove some men, particularly the Germans, to attempt the impossible on desperate climbs such as the North Face of the Eiger (the Ogre) in Europe and on other dangerous mountains such as Nanga Parbat in the Himalayas. The Eigerwand, as the great triangular, concave curtain of limestone forming the north-east face of the Eiger is called, rises above the valley of Grindelwald in full view of the spectators in the comfortable hotels. The tragedies that were played out on its grim, sunless face could not fail to make world headlines.

The first serious attempt on the Eigerwand was made in 1935 by two young Bavarian climbers who died in a storm at what became known as Death Bivouac. The following summer, two Austrian and two German climbers set out on what was to become one of the great tragedies of Alpine climbing. It was the year that the Olympic Games were held at Berlin; Hitler had announced that the first team to climb the Eigerwand would receive gold medals. The whole enterprise was permeated with nationalism and a desire to gild the romantic image of National Socialism.

The four men were all good rock climbers and Toni Kurz was both a qualified guide and a member of the German Mountain Regiment. By the third day they had reached a point just below Death Bivouac. The weather worsened next day and the four men were seen trying to come down. Hinterstoisser was setting up a difficult traverse, in reverse, because the climbers had retrieved their rope when they solved this problem on the way up. He failed and fell unroped to his death. Another climber, who already had a fractured skull from falling stones, came off at the same time and was strangled by his rope. His partner on that rope was hauled up close to a karabiner belay and died frozen to the rock face. The fourth man, Kurz, was left swinging by a sling midway between the two corpses, beyond the reach of a rescue party that had climbed out through one of the embrasures of the Jungfrau railway that winds up inside the face. After a stormy night, Kurz's left arm was frozen solid, but despite this he was able to follow instructions and retrieve some lengths of rope from his dead companions. These he unravelled with one hand and his teeth and joined together to make a single rope down which he could abseil.

The rope was 3 m (10 ft) too short and another piece had to be knotted to it. It was this knot that jammed in the karabiner that clipped Kurz to the rope. He died an ice-axe length away from his rescuers with his last words, 'I'm finished', spoken very clearly.

Two years later, in 1938, an Austro-German group made the first successful ascent. The Austrians were Heinrich Harrer and Fritz Kasparek. They set off on 21 July. The following day, after an uncomfortable bivouac, Harrer looked down the staircase of steps they had cut. 'Up it I saw the New Era coming at express speed; there were two men running – and I mean running, not climbing up it ... it hardly seemed possible that they had only started ... today.' These two were the German party consisting of Ludwig Vörg and Andreas Heckmair, both wearing the latest twelve-point crampons on their feet. The two parties agreed to climb together. During that afternoon Kasparek fell off and dropped 18 m (60 ft) before being held on the rope. When they bivouacked that night, as Harrer later recorded, 'the relaxed attitude of Vörg, the "Bivouac King" was quite remarkable. Even in a place like this he had no intention of doing without every possible comfort. He even put on his soft fleece-lined bivouac slippers, and the expression on his face was that of a genuine connoisseur of such matters.'

During the night Harrer slipped off his perch and awoke hanging by his rope in space. The next day an avalanche all but swept at least two of the climbers to their deaths, and the day after that, after another bivouac, Heckmair came off and was literally

Right: the Matterhorn in the Swiss Pennine Alps is one of the most striking mountains in the world, thrusting up like a great four-sided tooth into the blue sky. Here it is seen from the north-east with the Hornli Ridge in the centre. The Zmutt Ridge is on the right and the Furggen, the hardest ridge, on the left. The Italian Ridge is on the far side of the 4,476 m (14,688 ft) mountain. The first ascent by Whymper in 1865 was made by the Hornli Ridge and it is still considered the easiest way up, with fixed ropes at the more difficult part. It has in fact been climbed in as little as one hour three minutes.

The Italian Ridge was first climbed three days after Whymper's triumph and disaster, by his rival Jean-Antoine Carrel. The Zmutt ridge was first climbed in 1879 by Mummery but the difficult Furggen Ridge had to wait until 1911. Since then all the faces have been climbed.

caught by Vörg, whose hand was injured by Heckmair's crampon. When they finally reached the top in a howling blizzard it was so dark that Heckmair and Vörg just missed walking straight over the summit and plunging down the South Face. When in the end they all stood together on the peak the Austrians had been 85 hours on the face and the Germans 61 hours. Their route became known as the Original or 1938 Route. It has since been climbed many times, some of the conquests being solo attempts.

## Post-war Climbing

Since the Second World War, harder and harder routes have been attempted all over the world on faces that have already been climbed. Often these are so-called 'direct' routes going more or less straight up a rock wall. Two direct routes have been successfully climbed on the Eiger's deadly wall and it has been climbed in winter, and by women.

Elsewhere in the Alps the period since the war has seen an enormous increase in the numbers of people going into the mountains. The ski industry has boomed, together with other mountain sports such as trekking. In the Mont Blanc range alone there are more than 2,000 climbs and many of these have only been made possible by recent improvements in technique and equipment. As with all other competitive sports, the frontiers of the possible are continually being probed and pushed

even further out, and although there is now a reaction against the use of aids, such as expansion bolts, which made some of the new routes possible to begin with, the standard of climbing has improved so much that many such routes are now climbed without technical aids.

The Alps are now one of the busiest mountain areas in the world, but it is not all epic achievement. For every climber whose desire to make a 'first' drives him to the limit, there are hundreds of others who are content with the pure fun of climbing, of being in the mountains, face to face with rock or ice and a special, very personal sort of reality. There are also thousands of other visitors who would never dream of climbing, but who love and enjoy the mountains no less deeply.

If the early climbers were by and large well educated and well heeled, two World Wars have changed all that. The mountains have become a playground for the plumber and the bricklayer as much as for the teacher or the lawyer. Thousands of youngsters are taken to the mountains as part of their education, for the development of their characters as much as for the physical exercise.

Indeed, the mountains are now busy places and it is sometimes hard to find the solitude that was once thought so important. Climbers queue to attack the more accessible heights, ski lifts fill the valleys with their noise and smell, and civilization has come to some high

Above: Obergabelhorn, *left*, Zinal Rothorn and the famous Weisshorn, *right*, rising to the north above the Swiss town of Zermatt in the Pennine Alps. The Weisshorn, 4,504 m (14,780 ft), was first climbed in 1861 by Professor John Tyndall and the guide Johann Bennen. They climbed by way of the east ridge and on reaching the summit Tyndall later wrote, 'I had never before witnessed a scene which affected me like this one. I opened my notebook to make a few observations, but soon relinquished the attempt. There was something incongruous, if not profane, in allowing the scientific faculty to interfere where silent worship seemed the reasonable service.' This was from the man who resigned from the *Alpine Club* that same year when another noted climber, Sir Leslie Stephen, poked fun at 'those fanatics who . . . have somehow associated alpine travel with science.'

Right: the north face of Cima di Rosso, 3,366 m (11,043 ft), in the Bregaglia Alps, seen from the Forno glacier. The prominent rib on the face was first climbed in 1969 by Mark Springett and the outstanding British mountain photographer John Cleare, who took this picture.

tops in the form of revolving restaurants and litter. These developments worry many mountain lovers, since, as a result of man 'conquering' the mountains so thoroughly, both the peaks and the climbers have been changed. Deeply imbued with the romantic spirit, Geoffrey Young had written:

'If I could seal a hope for younger time,
climbers to come, then it should be for you
to know only two
verities, yourself and the hill you climb:
only two voices, the mountain's and your own.'

And: 'Solitude was essential for the creation of this mutual understanding with the mountains.'

Of course, not all of Europe is as crowded as Wales or the Central Alps with its ski centres and packaged tours. To the north lie the mountains of Scandinavia. In Norway, particularly, great efforts have been made to keep the mountains unspoilt. To the south lie the Pyrenees where the excellent climbing and ski touring have made less intrusive inroads into the wonderful mountain scenery.

## Eastern Europe

To the east, the great crescent of alpine mountains sweeps through Austria and then, with a short break, south through Yugoslavia and into the Balkans. A little to the north, the Alps merge into the foothills of the Carpathians which form another great crescent around the Hungarian plains, curving along the borders of Czechoslovakia, Poland and the Ukraine before turning into the heart of Romania. Further east still, stretching from the Caspian to the Black Sea, lie the Caucasus, every bit as magnificent as the Alps, with Mt Elbruz at 5,632 m (18,481 ft) some 900 m (3,000 ft) higher than Mont Blanc. Here the speciality is huge traverses over a number of summits. While western climbers are welcome, the Russian style of well-organized and closely controlled climbing is rather foreign to most of them.

Mount Ararat, 5,156 m (16,916 ft), with Little Ararat across the saddle to the left. The mountain is still venerated as the scene of Noah's deliverance from the deluge, and many attempts have been made to find his Ark near the summit, but without success. In the late 19th century the mountain, which now stands in Turkey, formed the junction of Russia, Turkey and Persia and the slopes of Little Ararat were a favourite haunt of bandits. Ararat soars nearly 4,300 m (14,100 ft) from these arid plains and is visible from 161 km (100 miles) away.

Above: the 'Throne of Zeus', the 2,888 m (9,570 ft) high summit of Mount Olympus in Greece. In eerie conditions like these it is not hard to see why earlier peoples were affected by the high and solitary mountain places and believed they were the haunts of gods, as well as demons, devils and spirits. Mountains have significance in many religions.

Left: a climber on the 'Dibona' route on the Cima Grande di Levaredo, 2,999 m (9,839 ft), in the Italian Dolomites. These magnificent towers of magnesium limestone are typical of the Dolomites which take their name from the French geologist the Maquis de Dolomieu, who visited the area in 1789 and wrote about the peculiar quality of the rock which climbers have since found so attractive. The Italian climber Emilio Comici made the first ascent of the north face of Cima Grande in 1933.

The Caucasus do, however, offer some of the finest mountaineering in the world. In the Tatra region of the Carpathians the same style of very long traverses has trained Polish mountaineers to be among the best. These mountains attract four million visitors a year and only *bona fide* climbers are allowed to stray off the well-marked trails.

South of the Caucasus lie the mountains of Turkey where Noah's arrival at the top of Mount Ararat was the first 'conquest' of any peak. 'It was accomplished in a combination of circumstances which is extremely unlikely to recur', wrote Francis Gribble in his book *The Early Mountaineers*.

While it was largely European climbers who pioneered the other great ranges of the world, the two World Wars have radically altered the sport. Not only did they largely kill the romance that was once felt, or at least its

expression, but they opened the way to more hazardous mountaineering by cheapening the value of a life. In the wake of Passchendaele, Auschwitz and Hiroshima *The Times* of London was not likely to ask 'But is this life? Is it duty? Is it common-sense? Is it allowable? Is it not wrong?' if a few men wanted to risk their necks on a mountain, as it had following Whymper's Matterhorn disaster.

On the plus side, the Second World War in particular greatly improved the science of survival and the equipment required. These developments have enabled men to climb, survive and even enjoy themselves in situations that would have been suicidal two hundred years ago. That in itself is a wonderful achievement. No less wonderful is the love of mountains felt by millions who ski, scramble, and trek, or simply savour some of the finest scenery in the world.

# NORTH AMERICA

The North American continent is a mountaineer's paradise. Its enormous range of terrain and climate provides every variety of climbing, from the Himalayan scale of the Arctic mountains, or the great rock walls of Yosemite, to the forested Appalachian trails. Skiing, too, ranges from the comforts and sophistication of the best resorts with their splendid snow conditions, to Nordic ski touring and mountaineering that verges on exploration.

Stretching in a great curving spine from Alaska to Mexico, the major ranges dominate the western side of the continent, forming the longest mountain system in the world. The central area alone, the Rockies, contains more than a hundred groups of mountains, each sufficiently well defined to warrant a separate name. To the east of this great spine the Colorado mountains overlook the central plains, while to the west the Cascades and the Sierra Nevada flank the Pacific coastal area, offering some of the most spectacular scenery.

At the start of the 19th century, much of this area was unexplored, let alone surveyed or climbed. Americans created their own mountaineering traditions in this more rigorous climate of exploration and survey. The opening up of a host of ranges and summits took place in three overlapping phases during the course of the 19th century, as the explorers moved westward.

The first western mountain climbers in North America were a party from the *conquistador* army of Hernando Cortés who in 1595 climbed the Mexican volcano Popocatepetl, at 5,452 m (17,888 ft) the fifth-highest summit in the continent. Cortés' reason for the expedition was partly to show the local Indians that nothing was beyond the powers of white men, and partly 'in order to find out the secret, where and how the smoke rose'. In addition, they found quantities of sulphur which they used to make gunpowder.

The first Anglo-Saxon mountaineer on record in what is now the United States was Darby Field. In June 1642 he set out with two Indians and in 18 days reached the summit of Mount Washington, height 1,916 m (6,288 ft), in the Presidential Range. Together with the Franconia Range these make up the White Mountains of New Hampshire. The local Indians he encountered at the base of the mountain 'accompanied him within eight miles (12·8 km) of the tip, but durst go no further, telling him that no Indian ever dared to go higher and that he would die if he went', wrote Governor John Winthrop.

This was an isolated ascent and none of the other peaks in the range were tackled until 1820, when Major John Weeks climbed and surveyed Mount Adams, Mount Jefferson, and Mount Madison.

During the first 30 years of the century, surveyors, often supported by local enthusiasts, climbed the main peaks of the Appalachians. Yet according to the Appalachian historian John Ritchie, when the Appalachian Mountain Club was formed in 1876 'the White Mountains were almost *terra incognita* to the residents of our New England cities'.

After the Louisiana Purchase of 1803 progress westward began in earnest. In a famous three-year journey, Meriwether Lewis and William Clark

Previous pages: the eastern portion of the magnificent Alaska Range, seen from the north across the Tanana River. The highest peak here is Mt Hayes, 4,216 m (13,832 ft). The range is subject to some of the worst weather in the world, but during the short summer the region is gay with Arctic poppies.

Above: the old gold-mining town of Ouray nestles in the lovely Uncompahgre Valley of Colorado, 'The Mountain State'. Not far away Mount

18 months of the Gold Rush. By 1889 a cog railway was taking sightseers to the summit.

Miners ascended at least six of the 'fourteeners', but the Indians had been there before them. Old Man Gun is known to have hunted eagles for their feathers on the summit of Longs Peak, at 4,345 m (14,256 ft).

The National Park in which Longs Peak stands together with a good part of the Front Range was established in 1915. The peak is the most important summit in the range and scrambling trails lead hundreds of hikers to the top each year, while the 550 m (1,800 ft) East Face towering above Chasm Lake boasts one of America's most famous big walls, the Diamond. This was first climbed in 1960 and is now a major classic, usually climbed free in two days.

The mountains of Colorado are high and blanketed with snow from December to May. Some of the best rock climbing has been developed on lower crags, notably Eldorado Canyon and the Black Canyon of the Gunnison, an inspiring chasm 32 km (20 miles) long and 610 m (2,000 ft) deep. Winter ice climbing on frozen waterfalls has been another recent development in the area.

Further north the famous 'Les Trois Tetons' (The Three Breasts) had been a landmark to trappers since the early 19th century, but it was only when the survey teams arrived that any attempt was made to climb them. In 1898 a local man, William Owen, with a colleague, M. B. Dawson, and their wives finally succeeded in climbing Grand Teton, height 4,196 m (13,733 ft). One 12 m (40 ft) long ledge known as the 'crawl' Owen described thus: 'as nice a piece of rock work as one would wish to see, and ... certainly not surpassed by anything in North America'.

The Tetons, situated on the Wyoming-Idaho border, are perhaps the most Alpine mountains in the United States. They are formed of an uplifted 'block mountain', mostly Precambrian rock, and moulded by repeated glacial erosion during several ice ages. The best weather for climbing is in July and early August.

Following Owen's 1898 climb, there was no further activity for some twenty years until the director of the nearby Yellowstone National Park invited in top climbers as part of a campaign to create a Teton National Park. This was done in 1929 and the park was later enlarged. The major peaks had all been climbed by 1931 and for the next ten years the Tetons were at the forefront of technical climbing in America; some twenty climbs were created. These range from the easy to American classics, such as the magnificent North Ridge.

The range has some of the atmosphere of the European Alps, the mountains being accessible and the climbing

Uncompahgre rises to 4,362 m (14,314 ft), a part of Colorado's San Juan Range that many feel to be the finest group in the state, with great variations in rock colour and form to please the eye. The Colorado Rockies are the highest part of the huge Rocky Mountain system outside Mexico, and have some 53 peaks over 4,267 m (14,000 ft), known as the 'fourteeners', and no less than a thousand over 3,050 m (10,000 ft). Much of the area was pioneered by miners during the gold rushes of the 19th century.

travelled up the Missouri and across the Rockies to the Pacific, exploring a territory almost double the size of the United States. While they were away Captain Zebulon Montgomery Pike led his pioneers to the foothills of the Front Range. In November 1806 they climbed what is now called Pikes Peak, height 4,300 m (14,109 ft), but it was the discovery of gold in Colorado in 1858 that made Pikes Peak famous. 'Pikes Peak or bust' became the rallying cry for the 100,000 immigrants who trekked west to seek their fortunes within the first concentrated in a relatively small area and well documented. Grand Teton is the most frequently climbed summit in North America, and elk, bear and moose are among the rich variety of wildlife enjoyed by visitors to this popular region.

## The Cascades

While the challenging peaks of the Colorado Rockies were being conquered one by one, and visits to the tops of the Appalachians were becoming almost tourist excursions, the spectacular mountains of the far west, the Sierra Nevada and the Cascades, were occupying the explorers. In 1792 the principal peaks of the Cascades were seen by Captain George Vancouver, but it was not until 1853 that the editor of *The Portland Oregonian*, Thomas J. Dryer, and three friends accomplished the first climb on one of the great Cascade peaks, Mount Saint Helens, 'The Fujiyama of America'. The following year Dryer climbed Mount Hood, height 3,421 m (11,225 ft). In the same year Mount Adams, 3,751 m (12,303 ft) high, and Mount Jefferson, 3,200 m (10,496 ft) high, were climbed, but Mount Baker, height 3,285 m (10,775 ft), remained unconquered until 1868 and Mount Rainier, height 4,392 m (14,408 ft), until 1870. The latter mountain, known to the Indians as Tahoma, soars more than 2,700 m (9,000 ft) in isolation above the forested highlands surrounding it. There are now some 40 separate routes up Mount Rainier, many of them very fine climbing.

The large mountains in this range are volcanic, four of them still showing signs of activity, and generally require only a hard scramble to reach the summit. By contrast, the 'North Cascades' of Washington are non-volcanic mountains, only two of which top 2,750 m (9,000 ft). The climbing offered here is exceptionally good but the weather is notoriously bad, and few mountaineers have attempted the major climbs during the winter months. In winter the snowfall is heavy and ski-touring is becoming popular. As elsewhere on the West Coast, the powder snow dropped by the Pacific winds rising up the mountains is legendary among skiers the world over.

## Sierra Nevada

One of the most famous of America's early mountaineers was Clarence King, who was exploring the Sierra Nevada before the last of the Cascades had been climbed. Stretching down from the southern end of the Cascades, the Sierras provide some of America's most beautiful scenery. Today much of the 640 km (400 mile) range lies within three national parks: Sequois, Kings Canyon, and the world-famous Yose-

mite. King joined the survey team of Professor William H. Brewer, and in 1864 set out with the party to explore the southern section of the unknown Sierras. They camped at Big Meadows early in July and Brewer climbed a peak overlooking the camp.

'The view was wilder than we have ever seen before', he wrote. 'Such a landscape! A hundred peaks in sight over thirteen thousand feet [3,960 m] – many very sharp – deep canyons, cliffs in every direction, sharp ridges almost inaccessible to man on which human foot has never trod – all combine to produce a view the sublimity of which is rarely equalled, one which few are privileged to behold.'

It is not surprising that he was excited, since he had expected to look eastward down to a desert. Next morning King set out with Richard Cotter, the two explorers taking with them provisions for a week. From the top of the ridge already named Mount Brewer they looked east across a 1,500 m (5,000 ft) canyon.

'Rising on the other side, cliff above cliff, precipice upon precipice, rock over rock, up against the sky, towered the most gigantic mountain-wall in America, culminating in a noble pile of Gothic-finished granite and enamel-like snow.'

They set off into this wonderland and by noon of the third day reached the summit – where King found an Indian arrow. 'I rang my hammer on the topmost rock; we grasped hands, and I reverently named the grand peak Mount Tyndall' – in honour of John Tyndall, whose book *Glaciers of the Alps* had so inspired King. Only then did King and Cotter see another, higher, peak 10 km (6 miles) along the rocky ridge, 'a cleanly cut helmet of granite . . . fronting the desert with a bold square bluff'. They dubbed it Mount Whitney in honour of their chief, Professor Josiah Dwight Whitney of the California State Geological

Right: Grand Teton, *centre*, the most popular summit in North America, rises above Valhalla Canyon. These superb granite peaks of the Teton Range in Wyoming, close to the Idaho border, rise some 2,000 m (6,562 ft) above the flats of the Snake River and Jackson Hole, which are themselves about the same height above sea level. Long ago fur traders and Indians used to rendezvous in Jackson Hole to talk and trade. The whole range is now enclosed by the Grand Teton National Park. On Grand Teton itself there are some 20 different routes to the 4,196 m (13,766 ft) summit which was first reached in 1896. The North Ridge of Grand Teton was climbed in 1931 and the North Face in 1936 by Jack Durrance and the Petzoldt brothers. This 850 m (2,000 ft) route, up the great 'fang' of granite, is still considered a fine climb, though it is not now considered tremendously difficult.

Below: the jagged but popular east face of Mount Whitney in the Californian Sierra Nevada. There is an easy track to the 4,418 m (14,494 ft) summit, but this east face offers the finest rock climbing, together with the spires on the left, Keeler, Day and Third Needle. Mt Whitney is the highest mountain in the USA outside Alaska. It is surrounded by five other 'fourteeners'. It was named in the 1860s by the most colourful of the early Sierran mountaineer explorers, Clarence King of the California Geological Survey. King made numerous first ascents but never managed Mt Whitney, although he tried several times.

Survey. It was later calculated to be 4,418 m (14,494 ft) high, the highest peak in the United States outside Alaska.

The Sierra Nevada was the last great obstacle in the old Overland Trail, and within its southern section it boasts many peaks above 4,000 m (13,000 ft) and 11 of more than 4,300 m (14,000 ft). The rugged summits tower above hundreds of small lakes and upland meadows famous for spring flowers. Great patches of naked white granite lend a special quality to the light.

Despite the heavy winter snowfall, the settled weather pattern of the Sierras and the multitude of peaks make this area one of the finest climbing areas for mountaineers of all standards. The trail system is excellent and in winter the country is perfect for ski touring and indeed winter climbing. The wildlife includes mountain lion, black bear and bighorn sheep.

## Yosemite

By 1863, the same year in which Clarence King made his first foray into the High Sierras, the fame of the Yosemite Valley, 177 km (110 miles) to the north, had spread so fast that Congress had to rush through an act to protect the valley from exploitation. The commission set up to put this into force needed a survey of the region. Professor Brewer was asked to allocate a man for the job. He selected Clarence King, who arrived in the valley that autumn.

Top: an American Black Bear investigates a beaver lodge in the mountains of Wyoming. America has several closely related species of bear, among them the Grizzly and the Brown Bears of the far north. The Black Bear is smaller and more common.

Above: a Bighorn or Rocky Mountain ram surveys his domain. This is the only wild species of sheep in North America and it prefers mountain country. It moves with rapid bounds, having soft pads on its feet to absorb shocks and provide grip.

Top: a Mountain Lion takes its rest. Originally these big cats, also known as cougars or pumas (*Panthera concolour*), were found from Alaska to Cape Horn. They are active at night and rely on stealth to catch their prey. They survive mainly in national parks.

Above: the North American or Rocky Mountain Goat is the only ruminant to keep its shaggy white coat throughout the year. It inhabits the craggiest and most remote mountain slopes, well above the tree line. It is only found in north-west USA.

Immediately he was struck by the geological interest of the 11 km (7 mile) valley, just as John Muir, the pioneer who started the National Parks movement was amazed at its beauty – 'too gentle to counter man's assaults against it'. King wrote:

'Nothing in the whole list of irruptive products, except volcanoes themselves, is so wonderful as these domed mountains. They are of every variety of conoidal form, having horizontal sections accurately elliptical, ovoid, or circular, and profiles varying from such semi-circles as the cap behind the Sentinel to the graceful infinite curves of Half Dome.'

Most of the major summits were apparently climbed by King and his companions, except for Half Dome, which was described by King as

'A crest of granite rising to the height of 4,373 ft (1,332 m) above the valley, perfectly inaccessible, being probably the only one of all the prominent points about the Yosemite which never had been, and never will be, trodden by human foot.'

Only ten years later, James Hutchings began his attempts on Half Dome, describing them later in a classic study of the Yosemite, *In the Heart of the Sierras*. Then in 1875 along came George G. Anderson, a Scots trail-builder and a man who spurned defeat, even by Half Dome. Having tried to walk up it in boots, then in stockinged

Above: the 'Nose' of El Capitan dominates the eastward view up Yosemite Valley. At its head in the distance stands Mount Watkins with the famous Half Dome to the right. In the right foreground are the backs of Cathedral Rocks near the Bridal Veil Fall. Here, with no objective dangers such as avalanches, and with predictable weather, philosophies and techniques for attacking such 'big walls' of rocks were developed which have profoundly influenced climbing the world over. Special equipment such as bolts, wide-angled pegs and tiny chrome-molybdenum knife-blade pitons, were developed and tailored to Yosemite's special conditions. After Warren Harding's 'Wall of Early Morning Light' ascent on El Capitan in 1970, with its 26 consecutive bivouacs and 300 bolt placings, there was some revulsion against the use of such 'aid' techniques and 'free' climbing without such aids has become the vogue. Climbing at Yosemite is typically fierce rather than enjoyable, but it remains popular with climbers and tourists alike.

Left: the awe-inspiring 900 m (3,000 ft) prow of El Capitan dominates the lower part of Yosemite Valley in California. The first ascent of 'El Cap' in 1958 took 47 days, spread over 17 months, using siege tactics and almost continuous aid. Today parties often queue up to attempt the 20 or so 'big-wall' routes on the face and, with much free climbing, four days is now the average time.

feet, then barefoot, then with sacking wrapped around his feet, he finally covered them with pitch from pine trees. Conjuring up a cartoon picture, he found he could adhere firmly to the smooth granite of the dome, but according to Hutchings, 'a new difficulty presented itself in the great effort required to unstick himself ... ' Then in a foretaste of things to come, Anderson 'procured drills and a hammer, with some iron eye-bolts, and drilled a hole in the solid rock; into this he drove a wooden pin, and then an eye bolt; and, after fastening a rope to the bolt, pulled himself up until he could stand upon it; and thence continued the process until he had gained the top – a distance of nine hundred and seventy-five feet [297 m].'

Others soon followed. It was here, with the help of the predictable weather, that technical rock climbing really started in the 1930s. Philosophies and techniques were developed which profoundly influenced mountaineering the world over.

The Valley, as the Yosemite is known, was carved by ice and water from the tilted granite block of the Sierras. A series of high and beautiful waterfalls cascade down the cliffs. The granite itself is compact and smooth, and climbing is usually long and fierce. The magnificent Nose of El Capitan, 900 m (3,000 ft) high, dominates the lower valley. The first ascent of El Capitan in 1958 took 47 days, spread over 17 months, the climbers using siege tactics and almost continuous aid – 700 pitons and some 125 bolts in all. Today climbers queue to attempt it and with a great deal of free climbing four days is now the average time. This

gives some idea of how rapidly standards have been raised.

There are more than 20 'big-wall' routes on the face. It was to tackle these and other big walls of the Yosemite that special pitons and hooks, such as tiny chrome-molybdenum knife-blade pitons, were developed by such men as the émigré Swiss blacksmith John Salathé. Great wide-angle pegs, Z-sectioned 'leeper' pitons, expansion and contraction bolts and nylon webbing were introduced here – equipment that soon became used throughout the world with greater or lesser enthusiasm. These techniques eventually led to a reaction against their over-use and many of the routes pioneered with technical aid are now climbed virtually free.

The reaction came to a head in the early 1970s, led notably by Yvon Chouinard, who was responsible for the introduction of so much of the equipment, with the exception of the bolt. Chouinard began a campaign for climbers to leave faces as they found them. Writing in *Ascent*, in the aftermath of Warren Harding's 27-day epic of the Wall of Early Morning Light on El Capitan in 1970, with its 300-odd bolt placings and 26 consecutive bivouacs, Chouinard crystallized the problem:

'Just as man continues to disrupt the natural order of things, so mountaineering has become increasingly technical, decreasingly difficult, much too crowded and far less venturesome. The purity, the uncertainty, naturalness and soul of the sport are rapidly being changed.

'Having been passionately committed to climbing for seventeen years, and with a business directly related to climbing and its problems, I feel a heavy responsibility to make known my apprehension over what climbing is becoming...

'I believe we have reached the point where the only hope is to completely degrade bolting. We must refuse to recognize it as a legitimate means of climbing...

'We are entering a new era of climbing, an era that may well be characterized by incredible advances in equipment, by the overcoming of great difficulties, with even greater technological wizardry, and by the rendering of the mountains to a low, though democratic, mean.

'Or could it be the start of more spiritual climbing, where we assault the mountains with less equipment and with more awareness, more experience and more courage?'

Within a few years, the tide was turning and a higher standard of free climbing became the vogue. During recent years there has been a return to the attitude felt so strongly by the climbers of earlier eras, that the laurels ought to go not simply to those who reach the summit first, but to those who do so in the right way.

However, the old rule that any pegs used are removed afterwards has caused terrible damage to fine cracks, and this has led to the development of 'nuts' which can be slotted into widened cracks like chocks. These leave almost no mark when removed and are commonly used now.

Although the mass of tourists that the valley attracts in summer rather spoil the peace, climbing in Yosemite is so popular that weekends see hundreds of climbers in action on the 500 or more recorded routes. As one of the old hands, Chouinard, wrote: 'Yosemite climbing tends to be difficult rather than enjoyable, but it possesses you with a passion that keeps bringing you back.'

Although Yosemite's fame is for offering the ultimate in rock climbing – an ultimate that is pushed forward year by year – it has also been a focus for the appreciation of the region's great natural beauty. John Muir was the first of many writers inspired by the valley, and countless photographers have tried to capture its spell.

The grant of the Yosemite Valley to California 'for public use, resort, and recreation ... unalienable for all time' marks the beginning of the National Parks Service. Because it is so attractive to so many disparate interests, from naturalists to rock climbers, it underlines the problem facing those responsible for wilderness areas the world over, of how to obtain the maximum value from an asset without spoiling it, and this is particularly difficult in a country where individual freedom is so dearly cherished.

Left: a bolt belay, *top*. A hole is drilled in the blank rock face and an expansion bolt holding an angled bracket is pushed in and screwed home. A snap-link karabiner is clipped into this secure position and the climber supports himself on it with a variety of webbing straps, hooks or *étrier* step ladders. On good rock the technique will take the climber around overhangs or vertical pitches where there are no hand- or foot-holds. Bolting is avoided whenever possible, partly because of the labour involved, but also because many climbers consider it 'unethical'.

A nut belay, *below*, is now often used. Many of the fine cracks at Yosemite were ruined by hammering in steel pegs or pitons, partly because of the old climbers' rule that pegs must be removed after use. Nuts, which do little damage, are now the most popular aid, but even these are eschewed by some devotees of free climbing.

Right: Lost Arrow Spire beside Upper Yosemite Fall, first climbed by A. Nelson and the Swiss blacksmith John Salathé in 1947 in a continuous five-day epic. Salathé invented the special hard steel pitons that made the ascent possible.

## The Far North

By the end of the 19th century, most of North America's mountains had been explored and surveyed, and the principal peaks climbed. Only in the far north-west were there ranges as yet largely unexplored and offering some of the finest unclimbed summits in the world.

Right at the north-west extremity of the great American mountain spine stand the St Elias, Fairweather and Wrangell mountains, and beyond them the Alaska Range, dominated by the colossal Mount McKinley, North America's highest mountain. From Anchorage, 320 km (200 miles) away on the Cook Inlet, the snow crest of the massif spreads across the northern horizon. In 1794 Captain George Vancouver, one of Captain Cook's officers, sailed up the inlet and wrote of 'stupendous mountains covered with snow and apparently detached from each other.' These were the mountains of the Alaska Range arcing for more than 645 km (400 miles) around the hinterland of the Gulf of Alaska. In spite of Mt McKinley's height of 6,194 m (22,322 ft), less than 20 of the other peaks exceed 3,000 m (10,000 ft). The

range has been called a crucible of evil weather and boasts sharp summits, enormous cliffs and spires heavily covered with snow. The largest and most important massif is Mt McKinley, called by the native Indians Denali – 'The Great One', or 'Home of the Sun'. It offers special problems to the climber, since it has the greatest height difference, base to summit, of any mountain in the world.

The mountain is Himalayan in scale and high altitude effects on climbers appear to be unusually severe. In what stands as one of mountaineering's most remarkable exploits, Mount McKinley was first climbed in 1910 by a party of Alaskan prospector 'sourdoughs', men with no technical climbing experience but accustomed to travel on snow and ice as part of their work. They succeeded in reaching the North Peak, dragging with them a 4 m (14 ft) flagpole. Their tale was treated with caution, especially after the disputed claim of the eminent explorer Dr Frederick Cook to have climbed Mt McKinley in 1906. However, in 1913, a fresh expedition tackled the mountain by the same Muldrow Glacier route, reaching the rather easier South Peak. Two miles (3·2 km) away on North

Previous pages: one of America's most awesomely beautiful mountains, Mount Huntington, 3,731 m (12,240 ft), stands just 11 km (7 miles) south of its highest, Mt McKinley. This pyramid of gracefully fluted ice and rock was first climbed by a French party in 1964 by the North West ridge, which is the one running down towards the camera. The West Face, climbed in 1965, is on the right and the face on the left in the shade of the heavily corniced ridge is the North Face, climbed alpine style by a two-man party in 1978. Snaking off into the far distance towards Cook Inlet, from where Captain George Vancouver RN first saw the Alaska Range in 1794, is the strangely striped Tokositna Glacier.

Left: Mount Assiniboine, the 3,618 m (11,870 ft) 'Matterhorn of the Rockies', is mirrored in the placid waters of Magog Lake. Like most of the Canadian Rockies it is built of uplifted and heavily glaciated sedimentary rock, which produces the marked stratification so typical of the range. There are several routes on Assiniboine, the classic one being up the icy North Ridge which faces the camera, first climbed in 1901. Moose, bear, mountain goat, caribou and wolf are plentiful in this part of the Rockies.

Right: the deep powder, bright sun and long slopes of Colorado: these are the skier's dream for which the mountains of the West are world famous. With winds off the Pacific Ocean bringing regular heavy falls of the finest snow, the great mountain backbone of America holds skiing runs for every taste and style among some of the most beautiful country in the world. Many of the developments, such as ski-lifts and trail groomers that have made modern skiing what it is today, were first introduced here; and as well as the sophisticated resorts North America offers the finest cross-country and ski mountaineering.

Peak they saw a roughly made American flag flapping in the wind. It later transpired that the 'sourdoughs' had reached the saddle between the two peaks and then chosen to ascend the wrong one – but their summit was only 91 m (300 ft) lower. The real victors took scientific readings and admired the view. 'The snow-covered tops of the remoter peaks, dwindling and fading, rose to our view as though floating in thin air when their bases were hidden by the haze, and the beautiful crescent curve of the whole Alaskan range exhibited itself from Denali to the sea', wrote the Archdeacon of the Yukon.

Bradford Washburn, who was closely associated with Mt McKinley since making the third ascent in 1942, wrote:

'... the ascent is a curious paradox. Under certain conditions it can be surprisingly easy, while under others it can be fiendishly difficult ... even the most powerful group may be forced to take a month or more.'

Despite this, the easy routes are now popular and regularly guided. The park authorities reckoned that 225 people climbed the West Buttress in 1976. Some dozen other routes have been climbed, including the magnificent 3,050 m (10,000 ft) South Face.

Mount Huntington, considered by many to be America's most savagely beautiful mountain, lies 11 km (7 miles) south-east of Mt McKinley.

These Arctic mountains are almost inaccessible except by air and are repeatedly underestimated by climbers not used to them.

The first ascent of a major peak in the far north-west was made by the famous Italian Duke of the Abruzzi who in 1897 succeeded in climbing Mount St Elias in the extreme south-west corner of the Yukon, for long believed to be North America's highest peak. The approach to St Elias required a difficult coastal landing, followed by a polar-style crossing of the long Seward and Newton glaciers before the Himalayan-scale ascent could begin. Conditions for the assault were ideal. At 5,000 m (16,400 ft) they halted for breakfast, admiring the huge bulk of Mount Logan, the world's most massive summit, shining in the sun. For some, breathing was already becoming difficult, but all ten men made it to the top, which stands 5,489 m (18,008 ft) above sea-level. 'No-one can describe that moment,' wrote Filippo de Filippi. 'Many of those men, who for thirty-eight days had struggled to stand the trying ordeal, sobbed like children. Their anxiety, their exhaustion, their palpitation, disappeared in that moment of enthusiasm.'

Mount Logan is the highest peak in the area, and at 6,050 m (19,850 ft) it is the highest mountain in Canada and the second highest in North America. It was not climbed until 1925. St Elias was not reclimbed for 49 years, and then with the aid of air drops. The continual bad weather makes this one of the most difficult mountains in the continent and few parties are successful. Many of the lesser peaks in the area are still unclimbed and only a few of the larger ones have been climbed twice.

To the south lies the Fairweather Range, named by Captain Cook along with Cape Fairweather because at the time he and his men had just endured a five day hurricane. As they charted the coast and hinterland, 'We continued to have most extraordinary fine Weather, with such gentle Breezes that we just crawl along shore', wrote one of his officers. The name has seemed a joke to later visitors, for the area suffers the foulest weather. These mountains are young and subject to earthquakes. With seven other mountains above 3,660 m (12,000 ft) the range is dominated by Mount Fairweather, at one time considered the most important unclimbed peak in North America. It was climbed in 1931, and the ascent was not repeated for 27 years. Today there are five routes on its ridges.

North of the St Elias mountains lie the Wrangell Mountains, the 'jewels of Alaska'. These are active volcanic mountains and provide technically the easiest summits in the region.

## Canadian Rockies

Stretching northwest from the US border, the Canadian Rockies form an almost continuous 720 km (450 mile) wall marking the continental divide, the high ground being rarely more than 80 km (50 miles) wide. The mountains are typically steep and spectacular, built of uplifted sedimentary rock, frequently limestones and shales which have been heavily glaciated and still hold a great deal of ice. They form huge towers and jagged fins and are nearly always well stratified.

There are more than 50 peaks topping 3,350 m (11,000 ft) and, travelling westward, the first sight of them is breathtaking. Hundreds of peaks stretch across the horizon like a glittering saw blade. Within the mountains there are many beautiful lakes and plentiful wildlife, including grizzlies, wolf and moose, as well as the tormenting mosquitoes. It is gorgeous country but much of it is relatively inaccessible. Early climbers were helped by the Canadian Pacific Railway and the first climbs were made at the beginning of the century.

Chief among the Canadian Rockies is Mount Robson, 3,954 m (12,972 ft). After six years of trying it was finally climbed by Conrad Kain in 1913, by

Above: the climber Bill March at work in the icefall of the Bugaboo Glacier. The Bugaboos lie in the northern Purcell Range in the south-east of British Columbia. Rising sheer from the glacier are a series of startling granite spires offering some of the best climbing in North America. The three main peaks are Bugaboo Spire, Snowpatch Spire and Howser Spire. Snowpatch Spire, 3,063 m (10,050 ft), was finally climbed in 1940 by its south ridge, having resisted many previous attempts.

Right: climbers tackle the intimidating 'Diamond' on the 550 m (1,800 ft) East Face of Longs Peak in the Front Range. This face, which rises above the sombre waters of Chasm Lake, is one of America's most famous 'big walls' and is now usually climbed free of aid techniques in two days. The mountain itself was climbed by Indians long before Europeans arrived. Old Man Gun is known to have hunted eagles for their feathers on its massive, square 4,345 m (14,256 ft) summit.

what is now called the Kain Face which has become a classic climb. The normal route is now on the southern flank which has a hut. Other climbs are the splendid 800 m (2,600 ft) North Face of steep ice, and the famous Emperor Ridge. The 1,524 m (5,000 ft) Emperor face of extremely steep ice was only climbed in 1978.

Mount Assiniboine, often called the 'Matterhorn of the Rockies' rises to 3,618 m (11,870 ft) from the meadows around Magog Lake, and is perhaps the most lovely summit in the Rockies.

Approaches are often long and difficult, except in the well-developed areas such as the Columbia Ice-Field, where there is also excellent skiing. For this reason great opportunities for new climbs exist.

Canada has enjoyed a boom in Nordic-style skiing and, although there are probably less than a million enthusiasts, the country offers some of the world's greatest skiing among the most magnificent mountain scenery. The potential for cross-country skiing is almost unlimited. Although there are excellent centres that cater for those who like prepared trails, the best skiing is for the adventurous, the Nordic rambler, the ski mountaineer and the lover of solitude. Another development has been the introduction of helicopter skiing in the Bugaboos and Cariboos, where small centres that can only be reached by chopper have been set up; these are surrounded by a vast wilderness of untracked mountain and glacier.

Since the Second World War, the Arctic mountains of Greenland and Baffin Island which faces it to the west across the Davis Strait have become interesting climbing grounds.

Although the climbing season here is very short and travel is as difficult as anywhere in the world, the summer weather is relatively stable and there is constant daylight. As with other remote areas, only modern air travel has made the area possible for climbers.

In Greenland the mountains ring the great ice cap, some of them rising up to 3,700 m (12,139 ft). The accessible peaks are now well known and mostly climbed, if only once, but literally hundreds of virgin peaks await visitors in the more remote parts and there are innumerable faces and spires of rock still to be conquered.

In Baffin Island most attention has centred on the Pangnirtung Pass on the edge of the Penny Ice-Cap at the south-east end of Baffin's mountain spine. A special feature of the area are the towers and rock walls rising thousands of feet from valley floors, usually composed of rough compact granite that provides perfect climbing. Like Greenland, the island has huge areas yet to be explored by climbers, and hundreds of unclimbed peaks to challenge those who can surmount the problems of reaching them.

Above: climbers with dog sledges approach Ingolsfjeld on the east coast of Greenland in spring. Since it was first reconnoitered in 1968, this 2,232 m (7,323 ft) tooth of rock has drawn a number of expeditions. The difficulties of travel in Greenland and the short climbing season kept climbers away until modern air travel made things a little easier. Even today the area is inaccessible, but 24-hour daylight and stable summer weather go some way to making up for this.

Right: the climber and photographer John Cleare *à cheval* on the West Ridge of Pigeon in the Purcell Bugaboos, a peak that is not far from the ice fall shown on page 50. The Bugaboos are the best known of the British Columbia mountains, partly perhaps because the peaks are easily accessible. They stand comparison with the finest rock routes in Europe and there is also magnificent skiing and trekking.

# SOUTH AMERICA

difficult climbing, but they involve a lot of snow and ice work and are splendid places to enjoy alpine-style climbing at high altitude without great difficulties with the weather, or with access.

The Cordillera Huayhuash and the Vilcabamba and Vilcanota, although similar to the Cordillera Blanca in height and difficulty, boast more extravagant ice formations, as well as more numerous ice avalanches. These areas were not major centres of mountaineering until the 1950s.

Between 1961 and 1970, approximately 1,100 Andean peaks were climbed for the first time, and also hundreds of new routes were forced on the more hazardous and interesting faces of those already ascended.

## Patagonia

Right down at the southern end of the continent lies Patagonia, a thousand-mile (1,600 km) tail to the continent that juts into the great Southern Ocean dividing the Pacific from the South Atlantic. The western side is a maze of islands, and steep fjords into which drop numerous glaciers. The coastal hills are cloaked with rain forest and dense twisted beech trees, and the region is almost uninhabited. Sweeping down close to this coast, the Andes are high and contain some of the most dramatic rock peaks in the world, draped in ice.

These are the Fitzroy group, named after Charles Darwin's captain on *The Beagle*, the Paine group, and the mountains of Tierra del Fuego, split off from the rest of the continent by the Straits of Magellan.

The highest summit is San Valentin, altitude 4,058 m (13,314 ft), in the Hielo del Norte, first climbed in 1952 by an Argentinian team led by Otto Meilung. The area contains a number of other peaks, including Cerro Aranales, 60 km (40 miles) to the south. The 3,437 m (11,277 ft) summit was first reached by a Japanese team in 1955.

The Fitzroy group is one of a number of groups on the Hielo Sur that are world-famous for their rock walls and spectacular spires plastered in verglas. A number of attempts were made on Fitzroy's great fin of rock before Lionel Terray and Guido Magnone were successful in 1952. Since then the mountain has been climbed by several routes, as have the surrounding peaks. One of these, the arrowhead of rock called Cerro Torre, which is crowned with an enormous mushroom of ice rime, was first claimed in 1959 by Cesare Maestri, but his ascent was considered doubtful because he returned delirious after his companion Toni Egger was killed on the descent. Later attempts failed, including Maestri's own controversial attack on the

Top: traders and donkeys negotiate a stony trail among the Huascaran Mountains in Peru's Cordillera Blanca, where over seventy summits top 5,490 m (18,000 ft) and eleven stand more than 6,100 m (20,000 ft) high. These summits and glaciers are the highest in the tropics and their ice-fluted faces have earned themselves a reputation for malevolence. In 1962 some 6,000 people died when a hanging glacier broke off from the northern flank of Huascaran and, during the 1970 earthquake, avalanches destroyed several villages, killing thousands of inhabitants as well as 15 members of a Czech expedition and a Chilean climber attempting the peak.

Facing page: the beautiful, ice-hung Nevado Huascuran Sur is the highest peak in the group at 6,769 m (22,208 ft).

Above: the awe-inspiring east faces of the Towers of Paine in Patagonia. Left to right are South, Central and North Towers.

and the Apolobamba. In the antiplano between these ranges and the Cordillera Occidental lies Lake Titicaca, at 3,811 m (12,505 ft) the highest large lake in the world.

The weather in the eastern ranges is less stable than that in the western ones, for in Peru the weather comes from the east and the jungles of the Amazon. The mountains of the Peruvian Andes are mostly high peaks of granite soaring up from dry uplands that are dotted with small lakes, and in spring swathed in wild flowers. All the high peaks are icy, and ice avalanches are a feature of the area, as well as some very destructive earthquakes.

In the Cordillera Blanca more than 70 summits top 5,490 m (18,000 ft), and there are 11 major mountains of more than 6,100 m (20,000 ft), including Huascarán, at 6,769 m (22,208 ft) the second highest mountain in America. The first major expeditions here were Austro-German parties who carried out the basic exploration in the 1930s. All the largest peaks in the area have been climbed, but there are still plenty of new routes to be explored. The mountains here do not always offer

# SOUTH AMERICA

Dividing South America geographically and politically, the Andean chain of mountains curves down the western side of the continent like a great backbone 8,045 km (5,000 miles) long. Stretching from north of the Equator to Cape Horn in the Southern Ocean, the Andes have as great a variety of mountain terrain as any range in the world and are considered by many to be the most beautiful.

The Andean crests run parallel to the western coast, rarely more than 160 km (100 miles) inland, while to the east their glaciers feed the headwaters of the great rivers of South America, the most famous being the Amazon, the River Plate, and the Orinoco.

As a climbing ground which has only become popular in the last few decades, the Andes contain the highest peak in the western hemisphere as well as some of the most challenging climbing in the world.

Throughout this vast mountain range there is evidence of early Indian civilizations, such as that of the Incas. Among the most impressive ruins are those at Machu Picchu, 2,440 m (8,000 ft) high on the Cordillera Vilcabamba, poised above the gorge of the Rio Urubamba, first visited by Hiram Bingham in 1911. In Peru the descendants of the Incas live as high as 4,876 m (16,000 ft), making a poor and often precarious living from their potato fields and herds of llamas.

Since many of the major peaks of the Andes can be seen from the towns on the Pacific coast, they did not require discovery as did the mountains of North America. However, like the summits of Europe, they remained simply a beautiful backdrop and were as little explored as the glaciers and upper snow fields of Mont Blanc. In 1802 the famous German geographer Alexander von Humboldt made attempts on both Chimborazo, height 6,267 m (20,562 ft), once thought to be the highest mountain in the world, and Cotopaxi, the highest active volcano in the world at 5,896 m (19,344 ft). He failed, and it was not until 1872 that the top of Cotopaxi was climbed by Wilhelm Reid.

In 1880 Whymper, of Matterhorn fame, mounted the first major mountaineering effort in the range, together with his old rival on the Matterhorn, the Italian guide Jean-Antoine Carrel. They made their first attack on Chimborazo and when they were above 6,095 m (20,000 ft) it seemed that the mountain was within their grasp.

'But at this point,' Whymper wrote, 'the condition of affairs completely changed. The sky became overclouded, the wind rose, and we entered upon a tract of exceedingly soft snow, which could not be traversed in the ordinary way. The leading man went in up to his neck, almost

out of sight, and had to be hauled out by those behind ... we found the only possible way of proceeding was to flog every yard of it down, and then crawl over it on all fours; and, even then, one or another was frequently submerged, and almost disappeared.'

For three hours they slogged on, and at 15.45 they at last stood on the western summit. It was the lower of the two.

'There was no help for it; we had to descend to the plateau, to resume the flogging, wading and floundering, and to make for the highest point, and there again, when we got to the dome, the snow was reasonably firm, and we arrived upon the summit of Chimborazo standing upright like men, instead of grovelling, as we had been doing for the previous five hours, like beasts of the field.'

Perhaps spurred on by Whymper's success, a German mountaineer by the name of Paul Gussfeldt attempted to climb Aconcagua, at 6,960 m (22,835 ft) the highest mountain in South America and indeed in the western hemisphere. He was foiled by the effects of altitude and bad weather, but in 1897 Edward A. Fitzgerald arrived with a party of Alpine guides. Fitzgerald, whose Canadian and American parents were extremely rich, was a rare man, even among mountaineers. The philosopher Bertrand Russell, who had climbed with him in Europe, wrote in his autobiography:

'He had been brought up in America and was exceedingly sophisticated. He was lazy and lackadaisical, but had remarkable ability in a great many directions, notably in mathe-

Pages 54–5: the remarkable shark-fin spires of the Fitzroy Group on the edge of the Patagonian-Heilo Sur ice-cap. The group is named after Captain Fitzroy, Charles Darwin's commander on the famous Beagle voyage. These diorite peaks are world renowned for the 'big wall' climbs they offer, compounded with the difficulties of verglas-plastered surfaces and ice-rime caps. The needle-shaped Cerro Torre on the left was climbed successfully in 1974 by Casimiro Ferrari's party. Earlier attempts and claims of ascent are doubtful. Fitzroy, 3,375 m (11,073 ft), is the highest peak on the right. Its ascent in 1952 by Lionel Terray and Guido Magnone was a milestone in climbing.

Left: throughout the Andes there is evidence of the earlier Indian civilizations that flourished among them. This is the site of the ancient Inca city of Machu Picchu, perched 2,440 m (8,000 ft) high on the eastern edge of the Cordillera Vilcabamba, above the swirling gorges of the Rio Urubamba. The city was rediscovered in 1911 by Hiram Bingham, and then only as the result of a chance remark by a local Indian. This was hundreds of years after the Inca empire had been destroyed by the 16th-century Spanish Conquistadors. The Inca empire stretched from northern Ecuador south into Chile and Argentina.

This 'Lost City of the Incas', as it was called after Bingham's discovery, is one of the most extraordinary sites in the whole of America, with some 13 square km (5 square miles) of terraced streets connected by more than 3,000 steps. The multitude of small houses are built of unmortared stone.

matics. He could tell the year of any reputable wine or cigar. He could eat a spoonful of mixed mustard and Cayenne pepper. He was intimate with Continental brothels. His knowledge of literature was extensive, and while an undergraduate at Cambridge, he acquired a fine library of first editions.'

Fitzgerald made four consecutive attempts on Aconcagua and failed. He suffered from the effects of unsuitable rations, high altitude, and the terrible cold. On the third attempt, Matthias Zurbriggen, the guide leader, made it to the summit. Fitzgerald wrote:

'Of my disappointment I need not write, but the object of my expedition was to conquer Aconcagua; I therefore sent Zurbriggen on to complete the ascent ... Three quarters of an

hour after he had left, I saw him four hundred feet (122 m) above me, going across the face of the big stone slope on the way to the saddle between the two peaks. Then for the first time the bitter feeling came over me that I was being left behind, just beneath the summit of the great mountain I had so long been thinking about, talking about, and working for ... I got up, and tried once more to go, but I was only able to advance from two to three steps at a time, and then I had to stop, panting for breath, my struggles alternating with violent fits of nausea ...'

In 1954 a French party led by R. Ferlet made the first ascent of the South Face of Aconcagua, in what has been described as one of the great feats of Andean mountaineering.

## The Peruvian Andes

For climbers, the Peruvian Andes have been the most attractive area of the entire chain, partly because they are accessible and also because they offer such splendid peaks. Rising steeply from the coast the ranges, or *cordilleras*, stretch north-west/south-east in a maze of interlocking groups. The Cordillera Blanca comes first in the area north of Lima, followed closely by the Cordillera Huayhuash. To the south, these fall away to several minor ranges extending for a distance of some 320 km (200 miles), in which the Nevado Huaguruncha rises to 5,729 m (18,797 ft). South again, a second ridge of mountains rises parallel to the Cordillera Occidental, known as the Cordillera Vilcabamba, followed by the Urubamba, the Vilcanota, the Aricoma

difficult climbing, but they involve a lot of snow and ice work and are splendid places to enjoy alpine-style climbing at high altitude without great difficulties with the weather, or with access.

The Cordillera Huayhuash and the Vilcabamba and Vilcanota, although similar to the Cordillera Blanca in height and difficulty, boast more extravagant ice formations, as well as more numerous ice avalanches. These areas were not major centres of mountaineering until the 1950s.

Between 1961 and 1970, approximately 1,100 Andean peaks were climbed for the first time, and also hundreds of new routes were forced on the more hazardous and interesting faces of those already ascended.

## Patagonia

Right down at the southern end of the continent lies Patagonia, a thousand-mile (1,600 km) tail to the continent that juts into the great Southern Ocean dividing the Pacific from the South Atlantic. The western side is a maze of islands, and steep fjords into which drop numerous glaciers. The coastal hills are cloaked with rain forest and dense twisted beech trees, and the region is almost uninhabited. Sweeping down close to this coast, the Andes are high and contain some of the most dramatic rock peaks in the world, draped in ice.

These are the Fitzroy group, named after Charles Darwin's captain on *The Beagle*, the Paine group, and the mountains of Tierra del Fuego, split off from the rest of the continent by the Straits of Magellan.

The highest summit is San Valentin, altitude 4,058 m (13,314 ft), in the Hielo del Norte, first climbed in 1952 by an Argentinian team led by Otto Meilung. The area contains a number of other peaks, including Cerro Aranales, 60 km (40 miles) to the south. The 3,437 m (11,277 ft) summit was first reached by a Japanese team in 1955.

The Fitzroy group is one of a number of groups on the Hielo Sur that are world-famous for their rock walls and spectacular spires plastered in verglas. A number of attempts were made on Fitzroy's great fin of rock before Lionel Terray and Guido Magnone were successful in 1952. Since then the mountain has been climbed by several routes, as have the surrounding peaks. One of these, the arrowhead of rock called Cerro Torre, which is crowned with an enormous mushroom of ice rime, was first claimed in 1959 by Cesare Maestri, but his ascent was considered doubtful because he returned delirious after his companion Toni Egger was killed on the descent. Later attempts failed, including Maestri's own controversial attack on the

Top: traders and donkeys negotiate a stony trail among the Huascaran Mountains in Peru's Cordillera Blanca, where over seventy summits top 5,490 m (18,000 ft) and eleven stand more than 6,100 m (20,000 ft) high. These summits and glaciers are the highest in the tropics and their ice-fluted faces have earned themselves a reputation for malevolence. In 1962 some 6,000 people died when a hanging glacier broke off from the northern flank of Huascaran and, during the 1970 earthquake, avalanches destroyed several villages, killing thousands of inhabitants as well as 15 members of a Czech expedition and a Chilean climber attempting the peak.

Facing page: the beautiful, ice-hung Nevado Huascuran Sur is the highest peak in the group at 6,769 m (22,208 ft).

Above: the awe-inspiring east faces of the Towers of Paine in Patagonia. Left to right are South, Central and North Towers.

and the Apolobamba. In the antiplano between these ranges and the Cordillera Occidental lies Lake Titicaca, at 3,811 m (12,505 ft) the highest large lake in the world.

The weather in the eastern ranges is less stable than that in the western ones, for in Peru the weather comes from the east and the jungles of the Amazon. The mountains of the Peruvian Andes are mostly high peaks of granite soaring up from dry uplands that are dotted with small lakes, and in spring swathed in wild flowers. All the high peaks are icy, and ice avalanches are a feature of the area, as well as some very destructive earthquakes.

In the Cordillera Blanca more than 70 summits top 5,490 m (18,000 ft), and there are 11 major mountains of more than 6,100 m (20,000 ft), including Huascarán, at 6,769 m (22,208 ft) the second highest mountain in America. The first major expeditions here were Austro-German parties who carried out the basic exploration in the 1930s. All the largest peaks in the area have been climbed, but there are still plenty of new routes to be explored. The mountains here do not always offer

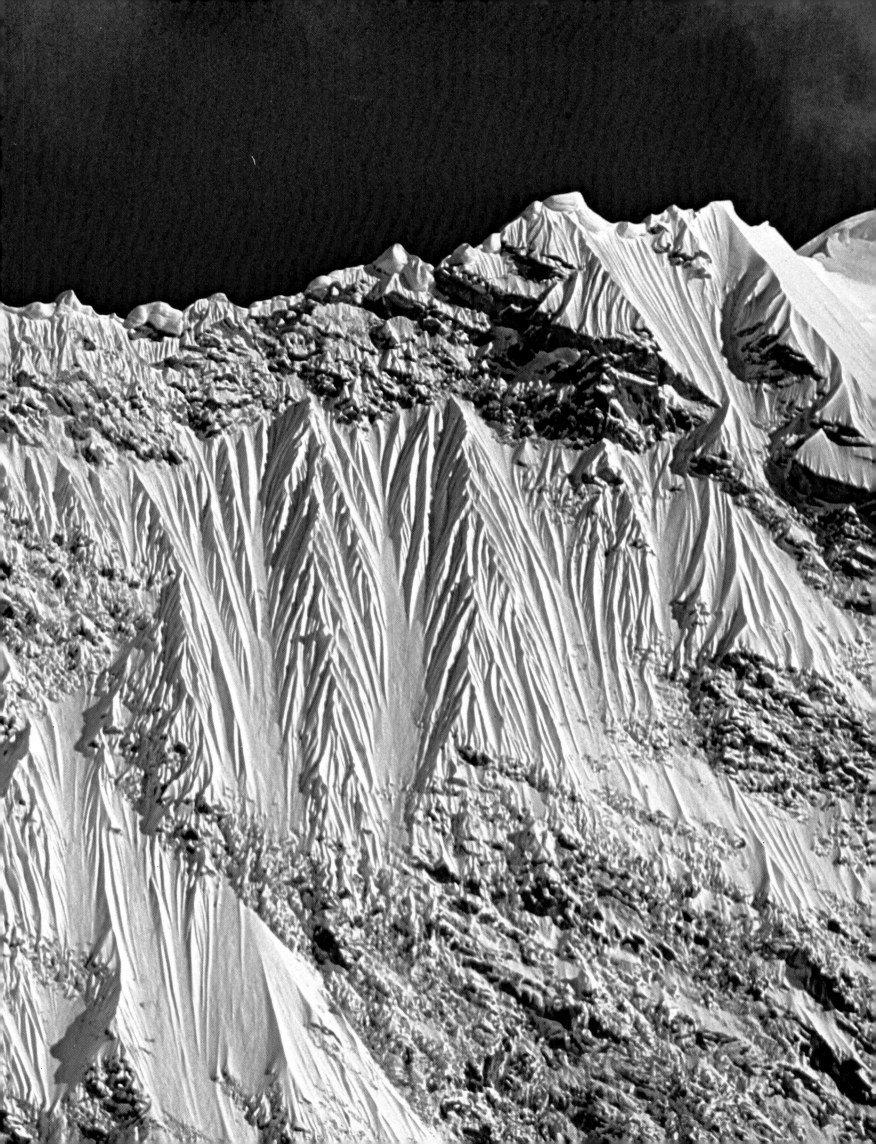

south-east wall using a compressor-driven drill and full aid tactics.

Finally, in 1974, Casimiro Ferrari succeeded in climbing the spire from the west in classic style.

A hundred and sixty kilometres (100 miles) to the south of this group, another spine of rocky spikes rises out of the flat arid plains of Argentina. This is the Paine Group, whose potential was not noticed by climbers until the 1950s. The main peak, Paine Grande, was climbed in 1958, and by the middle of the 1970s most of the principal summits had been claimed. The climbing here is invariably hard and the group contains some of the highest vertical rock faces in the world. These are now the focus of attention. In 1974 the 1,220 m (4,000 ft) East Face of the Central Tower of Paine was climbed by a South African team led by Paul Fatti, after a six-week battle.

Right at the southern tip of the continent, Tierra Del Fuego provides some adventurous climbing, with Mont Sarmiento and Mount Darwin rising to 2,472 m (8,110 ft). These strange and beautiful mountains, shrouded in mist and covered with ice, suffer spectacularly awful weather. Despite the fact that climbing conditions are limited to a few days in the year, several expeditions have visited the area.

As might be expected, the Andes offer something special to skiers as well as to climbers and trekkers. Portillo, some 150 km (93 miles) by road north of Santiago in Chile, has become a byword in North American skiing circles, not only because it provides skiing throughout the year, but it also hosts a Flying Kilometre world record week. The world Alpine Championships were held there in 1966. There are some nine other ski resorts in Chile and a favourite ski touring area is at Llaima, where there is an active volcano and rather exotic slaloming trails between dense monkey puzzle trees.

Top: Lake Titicaca, its shores shared between Bolivia and Peru, is the highest navigable lake in the world, at 3,811 m (12,505 ft) above sea level. In the foreground Aymara Indian huts stand on the Taraca Peninsular against the backdrop of Bolivia's Cordillera Real.

Above: the llama is closely related to the camel, but is smaller, humpless and has a long woolly coat. Along with its two near relations, the alpaca and the guanaco, the llama is used as a beast of burden in South America, and also provides, milk, meat and wool.

Left: the north-west peak of Yerupaja in Peru's Cordillera Huayhuash, taken from the Rondoy Pass. This splendid mountain is known locally as *El Carnicero* – The Butcher – but despite this tag it has received much attention from climbers since the area first came to their notice in the 1930s.

# THE HIMALAYAS

To all mountain lovers, the great ranges of Asia mean something very special. Their reputation as the highest, wildest and often the most dangerous mountains in the world is well earned. The names of the peaks themselves conjure up excitement – Kangchenjunga, Siniolchu, Annapurna, Everest, K2. Their reputation is one of awe-inspiring beauty and deadly fickleness. Like the countries in which they stand, Tibet, Nepal, Sikkim, they have about them an air of mystery, not least because in modern times they have been the scene of some of the most desperate and tragic climbing, as well as the most triumphant.

Stretching in a huge wall across the north of the Indian sub-continent, the Himalayas contain the highest and most difficult mountains in the world. They are mountains against which even the finest and most experienced of today's climbers may pit their wits and know there is a good chance of failure, or even death. For those who are not serious climbers, the areas that are politically accessible now provide some of the finest trekking anywhere in the world.

It is not only climbers and trekkers who are attracted to these magnificent mountains. For centuries the more passive, contemplative love of mountains has been a feature of the religions of the inhabitants of the region.

However, it was Europeans, with their drive to explore and to climb, who brought to Asia the active appreciation of mountains. The Himalayas had always been holy ground to the Hindus, and the Chinese made their seven holy mountains sacred to a Buddhist deity. Among these was Kailas, an unclimbed 6,417 m (21,054 ft) summit in south-east Tibet. Known in Sanskrit literature as the Paradise of Siva and Parvati, this mountain had for centuries been a centre for pilgrims who walked the 40 km (25 miles) circuit around it, through passes up to 5,486 m (18,000 ft). The very devout would do this circuit by prostrating themselves repeatedly – advancing about 1.5 km (1 mile) a day. This was about the extent of Chinese and Indian mountaineering, until Europeans took an interest in the Himalayas. But the respect that climbing such mountains engendered among Europeans was very deep.

Although the first climbers in the Himalayas were Europeans, the peoples of the area – of Turkestan, the Pamirs, the Hindu Kush, the Himalayas proper, the Karakorum, the Kun Lun and Tien Shan – these peoples had always been mountaineers, making a hard living from the steep valleys and crossing the passes when necessary, for trade, or because of war or famine.

As in America, at the start of the 18th century vast stretches of the mountain chain and of the high plateau of central Asia were unmap-

Above: the North Face of Everest, taken from base camp at 5,000 m (16,400 ft) by Captain J. Noel who was official photographer to the British expeditions of 1922 and 1924. This site at the foot of Everest's great Rongbuk Glacier was used as base camp by all the various expeditions to the north side between the wars. Apart from two unofficial attempts the whole of this side has been closed to Westerners since the Second World War.

The north route goes steeply up the Rongbuk Glacier to the North Col – on the left of the summit – and then follows the North East Ridge, or North Face, to the top.

In 1924 Edward Norton, who led the expedition, reached 8,572 m (28,126 ft) on the North Face without oxygen, only 274 m (900 ft) from the summit.

Previous pages: mighty Everest, on the left, with its characteristic plume streaming from the summit, with Nuptse and Lhotse on the right, seen from some 37 km (23 miles) away to the west at Gokyo Ri.

Top: the great ranges of the Himalayas were first mapped by the British as their Empire expanded its influence northwards into the mountains from India in the 19th century. This old hand-coloured photograph shows Major Moreshead of the Indian Survey making maps in hitherto unknown Tibet.

Right: Hidden Peak or Gasherbrum I, 8,068 m (26,470 ft) in the Karakorum. The shot is taken from base camp on the Abruzzi Glacier showing the South West Face. Hidden Peak is the world's number 14 mountain, and is so called because it is obscured by its great neighbours. It was first climbed in 1958 by the Americans Pete Schoening and Andy Kauffman. In 1975 it was climbed alpine style with only three bivouacs, by Reinhold Messner and Peter Habeler, taking the difficult and virgin North West Face. This breakthrough in high-altitude climbing was followed by their even greater triumph in 1978 when they climbed Everest without oxygen.

Facing page: the forbidding South Face of the world's second highest mountain, K2, which rises in splendid isolation in the central Karakorum to over eight km (five miles) high. Here the complex southern ice face soars 3,650 m (12,000 ft) above base camp at the head of the Godwin-Austen Glacier. The West Ridge is on the left skyline, while to the right falls the East Shoulder and Abruzzi Spur – known by that name since the ubiquitous Duke reached 6,700 m (22,000 ft) on it in 1909.

The real height of K2, which is the original survey number given to the mountain, is the subject of some doubt since the Pakistan Survey of 1974 reckoned it at 8,760 m (28,741 ft), only a couple of rope lengths short of Everest's stature, and 150 m (500 ft) higher than was generally accepted.

Top left: Pik Communism, formerly Pik Stalin in the Pamirs, is the highest peak in the Soviet Union. Here the rather inaccessible mountain is seen from the Valter Glacier. This craggy, 7,483 m (24,551 ft) high mountain has more than 15 routes on its various faces. Long, high traverses across several summits are a feature of Soviet mountaineering. One such 16 km (10 mile) traverse across Piks Garmo, Patriot, Russia, Communism and Pamir keeps climbers continuously above 6,100 m (20,000 ft).

Left: trekkers amble through the lush Kulu Valley in the Western Himalayas, famous for its orchards and flowers. Only 120 km (75 miles) from the Indian city of Simla, Kulu is the easiest range in the Himalayas to reach and is a wonderful place for small groups to enjoy both ski-mountaineering and alpine-style ascents. Wild peaks of rock and ice challenge the 'tigers' – or used to until they had scratched their claws on the best of it – and there are plenty of fine routes for the less zealous.

ped, and hardly explored. Even by 1920 only one European had been within 65 km (40 miles) of Everest. In addition, Sikkim to the south-west and Bhutan, Nepal, and Tibet to the north-east were long forbidden countries for Europeans. The era of exploration in the Himalayas coincided with 'The Great Game' of the 19th century as Russia seemed to pose a threat to British India.

The Himalayas stretch 2,410 km (1,500 miles) in a shallow curve across the top of India, 160–240 km (100–150 miles) in width, bounded to the east by the bend of the Brahmaputra River and to the west by the huge curve of the River Indus. To the south lie the fertile plains of India, to the north the high Tibetan plateau of Central Asia. West of the Indus the mountain structure continues as the Karakorum; further north-west still lies the Hindu Kush; and north again, inside the USSR, are the Pamirs. Then, curving back northeast for more than 1,150 km (700 miles), Tien Shan – The Celestial Mountains – stretch out towards Mongolia, for half their distance forming the present frontier between Russia and China. Among the thousands of mountains contained in these ranges more than 30 rise above 7,620 m (25,000 ft) and more than a dozen above 7,925 m (26,000 ft), with Everest the highest in the world at 8,848 m (29,028 ft).

The first Europeans to visit these regions were probably the men of Alex-

Top left: the weekly market for Sherpas and Bhotiyas (Tibetans) at Namche Bazar, 3,413 m (11,200 ft) up in the Khumbu region of Nepal. The Bazar is the 'capital' of Khumbu and is reached by a 13-day march from Lamosangu, itself a three-hour drive on the 'Chinese Road' from Kathmandu. The region is now a National Park; and the friendly Sherpa people, with their neat villages set among steep peaks and open pastures, have made this the Himalayan trekker's Mecca.

Left: paying out the porters during an expedition in Nepal. The porters are employed by expeditions to carry loads either to base camp or on the mountain itself. The peaceful Sherpas are the most famous porters, and were used on the first Everest expeditions. They quickly developed into expert mountaineers in their own right, many becoming 'high-altitude porters' – a much prized position. Sherpa Tenzing Norgay, who made the first ascent of Everest with Hillary, is the most famous of these men, and his triumph gave an enormous fillip to Asian mountaineering.

Right: the gorge of Kali Gandaki in Nepal with 'chortens' in the foreground.

ander the Great's army who crossed the Indus in about 328 BC. Communities said to descend from stragglers of this army still inhabit some of the remotest valleys of Nuristan, an area of the Hindu Kush north of the Khyber Pass.

Other travellers, such as Marco Polo, described the parts of the ranges that they saw. Polo took the old silk road through the Pamirs to China in 1273. For 1,126 km (700 miles) between Kashgar and Turfan the road passes along the edge of the Takla Makan desert, while to the north the Celestial Mountains of Tien Shan fill the horizon with their ice-bound summits. To this day one of the breeds of large mountain sheep found in the region is named *Ovis poli* after Marco Polo who first described it.

The first explorations of the Himalayas came at about the time that Mont Blanc in Europe was first climbed, but for very different reasons. The extension of British power in India brought Pax Britannica to the foothills of the Himalayas and into Nepal and the Punjab. With this extension of British power came the need for a survey. The Survey of India which was expanded to cover the new mountain areas was largely manned by military officers. As the survey pressed deeper into the mountains, sometimes with survey stations as high as 6,100 m (20,000 ft), various explorers and scientists arrived too. Often these men pressed on beyond the range of British protection, mapping huge areas of unexplored territory.

Not until 1892 did a real mountaineering expedition arrive in India, led by Martin Conway, and including among its members Charles Bruce, five Gurkhas from his regiment and the alpine guide Matthias Zurbriggen. The party surveyed the Baltoro, Hispar and Biafo Glaciers in the Karakorum and climbed a number of sizable peaks.

The first Himalayan disaster to catch public attention occurred in 1895 when A. F. Mummery's expedition attempted to conquer Nanga Parbat, at 8,125 m (26,658 ft) the ninth highest mountain in the Himalayas. It was a mountain that was to acquire a particularly omi-

nous reputation in years to come. Mummery, who was one of the finest alpine climbers of his day, reached about 6,095 m (20,000 ft) on the northwest face. He believed he could reach the summit from there in one day. On 23 August he and two of Charles Bruce's Gurkhas set off to cross from the Daimir to the Rakhiot Glacier. They were last seen the following day, and were probably overwhelmed by an avalanche.

Bruce, who was to lead subsequent attempts on Everest, learned two essential lessons from this disaster: first, that special food was necessary above 6,095 m (20,000 ft); second, that you cannot rush a 7,924 m (26,000 ft) peak from 6,095 m (20,000 ft). It was Bruce who first sensed that the Gurkas had the potential to become skilled western-style mountaineers. From this sprang the use of Sherpas on the first Everest expeditions and the creation of a group of elite porter/climbers.

By the turn of the century, there were expeditions almost every year to the various ranges. Through trial and

error, knowledge of how to climb successfully in the Himalayas was being accumulated, and techniques that had recently been successful in the Alps were tried out and modified to suit the enormous scale of Himalayan mountains. The meteorology of the monsoon seasons, which govern success or failure of attempts on almost all the ranges, was becoming better understood. The charms as well as the dangers of the Himalayas were becoming known.

Describing a dawn on his first visit to the Himalayas, Hugh Merrick wrote a typically lyrical account.

'At Sandakphu next morning in a bitterly cold and cloudless dawn, we stood transfixed as a new day surged across two hundred miles of the earth's backbone. Westward, suddenly, by virtue of a thousand foot pre-eminence over all else in the sleeping world, Everest's remote blunt head glowed solitary, for long minutes, like a living coal in the lilac of the morning sky. One after another, then, by precedence of altitude, a dozen mighty crests caught fire; gradually the fretted slopes below them were consumed by the slowly descending lava of crimson, orange and gold, till a hundred treasures of the Himalaya stood sunlit and serene to the morning. Ten thousand feet below our vantage point, blue gulfs as yet unpenetrated by the light of day, slumbered the abysmal valleys of Nepal. And, miracle of all those icy miracles – a great asymmetrical pyramid of snow, ice and palest dove-grey granite, completely dwarfing its mighty neighbour Jannu – Kangchenjunga swept and soared in indescribable magnificence, still more than all Mont Blanc's sea-level stature above our heads.'

## The Ascent of Everest

The story of climbing in the Himalayas demonstrates again how important is the accumulation of experience in overcoming a difficult problem. The ascent of Everest is typical of this gradual improvement in knowledge, equipment and technique.

In May 1921 a party led by Colonel C. K. Howard-Bury, including nine British climbers, among them George Mallory and Guy Bullock, together with 40 Sherpa porters, set out from Darjeeling to explore the area and to discover a route to the top of Everest. They climbed as high as the North Col on the northern side of the mountain, which was to be the approach of the seven British attempts on Everest before the Second World War. Here, at a height of 6,984 m (22,916 ft), they could see the slopes of the north face and experienced Everest's terrible west wind. Mallory wrote:

'And higher was a more fearsome sight. The powdery fresh snow on the great face of Everest was being swept along in unbroken spindrift and the very ridge where our route lay was marked out to receive its unmitigated fury. We could see the blown snow deflected upwards for a moment where the wind met the ridge, only to rush violently down in a frightful blizzard on the leeward side. To see, in fact, was enough; the wind had settled the question; it would have been folly to go on ...'

The expedition had been a success, however, for the party had discovered a route at least as far up as the North East Shoulder, about 8,381 m (27,500 ft) high, from which it might be possible to reach the summit itself. The climbers had also surveyed a huge area of the surrounding territory and learned a great deal about human endurance and local weather conditions.

The next year another expedition was mounted, equipped with open-circuit oxygen apparatus and led by General Charles Bruce, a man much loved by the Gurkha and Sherpa hill-

Above: the wild Rashi Gorge defeated climbers until Eric Shipton, Bill Tilman and three Sherpas forced their way through in 1934.
Right: the terraced hills of Nepal above Lamosangu on the second day of the approach march to Everest.

men. On this attempt Geoffrey Bruce, a cousin of the general, and George Finch reached 8,229 m (27,300 ft) on the north-east ridge, but the expedition was later abandoned after an avalanche killed seven Sherpas.

The use of oxygen was very much an experiment. It was heavy, but it was hoped that it would solve the problem of breathing at high altitude where the air is thinner. The debate as to whether it was 'sporting' or not was just beginning; Mallory thought it was a 'damnable heresy'. What was important in later expeditions was the gradual improvement in the equipment so that the balance between its usefulness and its weight gradually tipped in favour of its usefulness. The early sets were too heavy and were often as much a hindrance as a help.

There was no attempt in 1923, but

Top: a lovely rhododendron in Bhutan.

Above centre: a youngster practising archery, the national sport of Bhutan, with Thimphu dzong (fortress) behind.

Above: a Bhotia woman milks her yak, in east-central Nepal near the Lamjura Pass.

Left: the final section of Brammah I in the rarely visited Kishtwar Himal. It was first climbed in 1973 by Chris Bonington and Nick Escourt, who made an important breakthrough by climbing a fairly big Himalayan peak, 6,410 m (21,000 ft), in Alpine style.

the following year another British expedition was mounted. Originally led by General Bruce, who was taken ill, it was led by Edward Norton, following a plan evolved largely by Mallory. Three attempts were made on the summit, Norton himself reaching 8,572 m (28,126 ft) – within 274 m (900 ft) of the summit – without oxygen, and while still exhausted from the calamities the previous weeks when blizzards had torn the expedition's well-laid plans to shreds.

'I feel I ought to record the bitter feelings of disappointment which I should have experienced on having to acknowledge defeat with the summit so close', Norton wrote in *The Fight For Everest, 1924.* 'Yet I cannot conscientiously say that I felt it much at the time. Twice now I have had thus to turn back on a favourable day when success had appeared possible, yet on neither occasion did I feel the sensations appropriate to the moment. This I think is a psychological effect of great altitudes; the better qualities of ambition and will to conquer seem dulled to nothing and one turns downhill with but little feelings other than relief that the strain and effort of climbing are finished.'

Mallory and 22-year-old Andrew Irving made the third attempt – using oxygen. They never returned, and were last seen by N. E. Odell – 'There was a sudden clearing of the atmosphere above me,' he later wrote, 'and I saw the whole summit ridge and the final peak of Everest unveiled. I noticed far away on the snow slope leading up to what seemed to me to be the last step but one from the base of the final pyramid, a tiny object moving and approaching the rock step. A second object followed and then the first climbed to the top of the step.'

What happened to the two men was never discovered. Whether they reached the summit before some accident occurred is an unanswered riddle. No trace was found until 1933 when an ice axe that could have belonged to either of them was found at about 8,412 m (27,600 ft).

Of the next five British expeditions that attempted Everest before World War Two none got any further than Norton had done. However there was a reaction against the enormous official expeditions with their hundreds of porters. Although small parties travelling light, living largely off the land, might not be able to manage Everest, there were literally hundreds of other peaks that would give as good sport – if it was sport a climber was after. No further approach to Everest was allowed until 1933.

The years between the two World Wars were a time when nationalism entered the sport in extreme form, par-

ticularly among the German climbers. Paul Bauer led two determined German expeditions to Kangchenjunga in 1929 and 1931, and in each the descent became an epic of endurance, as bad weather bringing blizzards and deep snow caught them high on the ice ridge above the Zemu glacier. The mountain was not climbed until 1955.

While there were dozens of expeditions throughout the great ranges of Asia between the wars, including important climbs by the Americans, the French and the Japanese, two major series of expeditions dominated the scene between 1932 and the declaration of war, those of the Germans on Nanga Parbat and those of the British on Everest.

Nanga Parbat, height 8,125 m (26,658 ft), stands at the western end of the Great Himalayan chain and rises 7,010 m (23,000 ft) from the arid valleys of the Indus and Astor rivers. It is one of the grandest peaks in the world and has a well-earned reputation for being one of the most difficult of all mountains, having claimed the lives of some 32 climbers. It has three flanks, falling from a 24 km (15 mile) crest. The Rupal Flank or South Face of Nanga Parbat, dropping 4,500 m (14,800 ft) from the summit to the desert of ice and rock below, is considered to be the highest mountain face in the world. It was first climbed in 1970 by Reinhold Messner, who was later the first man to climb Everest without oxygen, and his brother Gunther, who died in an avalanche on the descent.

Thirty-seven years after Mummery disappeared, a small German expedition led by Willy Merkl established seven camps during July 1932, reaching 6,955 m (22,820 ft) before the weather broke.

In 1934 Merkl was back, but the expedition was a disaster. One man died of pneumonia while the lower camps were being pitched. The expedition got within four or five hours of the summit, they estimated, when the weather broke again. No less than 16 men had to fight their way down from Camp VIII in the teeth of a blizzard. The next three camps had been swept away. Three of the German climbers died, including Merkl, and six Sherpas.

The Germans were back on Nanga Parbat three years later, led by Dr. Karl Wien. This time the mountain gave advance warning of danger, sending down an avalanche that nearly wrecked Camp II. However, the party pushed on up to Camp IV which was to be the assault base. On 18 July Uli Luft climbed up from Base Camp to join the rest of the party at Camp IV. He found the camp completely buried by an avalanche, with neither tents nor men visible. Seven climbers and nine porters had died. Despite this tragedy, one of the worst in the history of climbing, the Germans made two more

attempts on Nanga Parbat before war brought all climbing to a halt.

After the war Nanga Parbat was climbed by Hermann Buhl in one of the most extraordinary feats in mountaineering history. In 1953 a strong German party tackled the mountain and again met with terrible weather. On 3 July, with his companion too exhausted to go on and after the assault had been called off by the leader at Base Camp, Buhl left the top camp, V, at 02.30 alone. By 19.00 he was at the summit.

'Nothing went up any further, anywhere. There was a small snow-plateau, a couple of mounds, and everything fell away on all sides from it ... There I was on that spot, the target of my dreams, and I was the first human being since creation's day to get there. But I felt no wave of overmastering joy, no wish to shout aloud, no sense of victorious exaltation. I had not the slightest realization of the significance of that moment. I was absolutely all in.'

After ten minutes, Buhl began the descent. Almost immediately he lost the strap of a crampon, and it took him two hours to descend 137 m (450 ft). About 21.00, night closed in. There was nowhere to sit down and he stood through the hours of darkness on a narrow ledge wearing a wind jacket and a thin pullover. It was the highest open air bivouac ever made at that time. Fortunately the night was calm. When the moon came up at 04.00, Buhl continued the descent, plagued by hunger, thirst and cruel hallucinations of rescuers. After 40 hours on the mountain he finally saw two real men coming to his aid. Tragically, only four years later Buhl was killed on Chogolisa in the Karakorum.

After the Second World War the chances of successfully climbing Everest were greatly improved. The demands of war led to the development of much better oxygen equipment, while rope, clothing, boots and sleeping equipment were immeasurably improved by the introduction of man-made fibres. Portable radios allowed good communications even in bad weather, and scientifically designed food packages contained maximum nourishment for much less weight. It was largely due to these improvements, as well as to the accumulation of knowledge and experience, that led to success on the highest mountains in the immediate post-war years.

The situation on Everest was altered further by the political circumstances of the area. First the Tibetans had refused to allow mountaineering parties into the country, then the Chinese occupation made the chances of entry even less likely. Finally, the Nepalese authorities decided to admit mountaineers, thus opening up the southern approach to Everest that had hardly been considered before.

It was the French who in 1950 achieved the first post-war success in the Himalayas with their ascent of Annapurna, which at 8,078 m (26,504 ft) was the first of the mountains over 8,000 m (26,248 ft) to be climbed and the highest then climbed by man. This was achieved by an outstanding team of French guides and amateur climbers led by Maurice Herzog. Louis Lachenal and Herzog reached the summit in good weather but tired out. The descent developed into a nightmare journey. Eventually the entire party got down, but Lachenal lost all his toes from frostbite, while Herzog lost fingers and toes, and was lucky to lose only those.

While the French were tackling Annapurna, an American and British party was making a reconnaissance of Everest from the south. The following year, another party, which included the New Zealander Edmund Hillary, solved the problem by finding a likely route on this south side.

Finally, in 1953, a British party led by Colonel John Hunt, now Lord Hunt, achieved the perfect combination by placing climbers in the right place to make a summit attempt, at the right meteorological time, and in the right physical condition. The team was a strong one and the organization superb.

The first summit party, consisting of

Above: Sherpas pondering unexplored country in Nepal.

Above left: Dougal Haston at Camp 5 on the South Face of Annapurna. Annapurna II, 7,937 m (26,041 ft), is the sharp pointed peak in the central background. Annapurna I, 8,078 m (26,504 ft), was the first peak over 8,000 m to be climbed and the first great climb in Nepal. The epic ascent by a French team in 1950 took a terrible toll in frostbitten fingers and toes. The 1970 attempt on the 2,740 m (9,000 ft) South Face was a milestone in Himalayan climbing. The British expedition led by Chris Bonington put Don Willans and Dougal Haston on the summit.

Tom Bourdillon and R. C. Evans, climbed to the south summit. Beyond them they had only a narrow crest stretching some 457 m (500 yds) to the true summit which was only 91 m (300 ft) higher. However their oxygen equipment was giving trouble and already it was 13.00. Reluctantly they turned back, having climbed higher than any man had before.

Two days later, on 29 May 1953, the second summit attempt was made by Edmund Hillary and the Sherpa Tenzing Norgay. Tenzing was the ideal Sherpa for the job, for he had been on almost every Everest expedition in the previous 18 years, in addition to many other Himalayan ascents. By 09.00 they were on the South Peak and set off along the ridge, cutting steps.

'I was beginning to tire a little now', Hillary wrote later. 'I had been cutting steps continuously for two hours, and Tenzing, too, was moving very slowly. As I chipped steps around still another corner, I wondered rather dully just how long we could keep it up. Our original zest had now quite gone and it was turning more into a grim struggle. I then realized that the ridge ahead, instead of still monotonously rising, now dropped sharply away, and far below I could see the North Col and the Rongbuk glacier. I looked upwards to see a narrow snow ridge running up to a snowy summit. A few more whacks of the ice-axe in the firm snow and we stood on the top.

'My initial feelings were of relief — relief that there were no more steps to cut — no more ridges to traverse and no more humps to tantalize us with hopes of success.'

It was 11.30. The two climbers shook hands and thumped each other on the back, and took photographs. Then Tenzing made a small hole in the snow and put in a small gift of food for the Gods which the Buddhists believe live on the summit. Hillary made another hole and put in a crucifix which Hunt had asked him to take. By early afternoon they were back with their friends and it was all over.

Summing up in his book *The Ascent of Everest* published after this triumph in mountaineering, Lord Hunt wrote:

'Ultimately, the justification for climbing Everest, if any justification is needed, will lie in the seeking of their "Everests" by others, stimulated by this event as we were inspired by others before us.'

## After Everest

The ascent of Everest marked a watershed in the climbing world. It was not just that two men had stood on the highest summit in the world. One of them was the Sherpa Tenzing Norgay. Tenzing's triumph echoed through the non-European world, particularly India.

Since then Everest and the other great peaks of Asia have been climbed by men and women from many nations, including Indians, Chinese, Russians and Japanese. Everest itself has been climbed from north and south and by its southwest face; it has been climbed by women; and men have skied down from its South Col. Finally, in May 1978, it was climbed without oxygen by Peter Habeler and Reinhold Messner, proving once and for all that any mountain can be climbed without this aid.

# AFRICA

Africa boasts no great spine of mountains and no massive ice-bound ranges, as do other continents. Her ranges are relatively small, and her highest mountains isolated, separated from each other by thousands of square kilometres of desert, jungle, and savannah that is world famous for its wildlife and spectacular scenery.

The main ranges in Africa are the Atlas in the north-west of the continent, the Ethiopian highlands in the east, and the series of ranges in southern Africa that skirt the high interior plateau within 240 km (150 miles) of the southeast coast, from Cape Town to Natal. In addition, in the centre of the Sahara Desert rise two small and relatively low ranges of arid mountains, the Ahaggar and the Tibesti. However, the grandest mountains in Africa are not part of ranges but rise in isolation. Within 16 km (10 miles) of the Equator, Mount Kenya soars to 5,199 m (17,085 ft) from the high surrounding moorland. Due south of Mt Kenya, some 320 km (200 miles) away, rises the highest mountain in Africa, Mount Kilimanjaro, 5,895 m (19,340 ft) high. Like Mount Kenya it is a dormant volcano, one of the biggest in the world and unusually isolated for such a large peak. Also almost on the Equator, and 828 km (515 miles) west of Mt Kenya, lie the Ruwenzori, once known as the 'Mountains of the Moon' and one of the sources of the Nile waters. This is a small range rising out of the Western Rift Valley. Mount Stanley, its highest peak, reaches a height of 5,109 m (16,763 ft) and was named after the famous explorer who in 1876 was the first European on record to glimpse its eternal snows.

## The Atlas Mountains

The Atlas Range stretches across north Africa from Morocco to Tunisia. Much of the eastern part is simply high plateau, although there are small clumps of hills and mountains that make pleasant trekking. The western half of the chain, which lies in Morocco, is divided into three ranges running parallel to Morocco's Atlantic coast in a northeast/southwest direction. Of these, the central range known as the High Atlas is of the most interest to climbers. The local inhabitants are not Arabs but Berbers, an independent and picturesque people who wrest a hard living from their beautiful surroundings. The area is subject to great variation in weather, the summers being extremely hot and dry while the winters bring heavy snow to the mountains. In spring, particularly, the area is very beautiful, with wild flowers and orchards in full bloom, the streams full and sparkling and the trees and maize terraces a rich green.

The High Atlas contains a dozen

peaks topping 3,900 m (13,000 ft), but the main attention from climbers has centred on the highest group, the Massif du Toubkal, which reaches 4,165 m (13,600 ft). The rock of the Massif is volcanic in origin and varies in quality, frequently being poor on the south side while the peaks tend to be imposing rather than elegant, with steep rock faces. The two good climbing periods in the area are spring and winter. The other areas of the Atlas have attracted less attention from climbers, principally because they often require long approaches. On the other hand, this feature makes the area excellent for ski-touring and trekking.

## Mount Kenya

Mount Kenya is the eroded remains of a great volcano, estimated to have once topped 7,010 m (23,000 ft). Glaciers have now worn it down to a height of 5,199 m (17,085 ft) but, rising in isolation from the surrounding bush and often visible from more than 160 km (100 miles), it is a very distinctive peak.

The summit itself is the old plug of the volcano, consisting of some 609 m (2,000 ft) of steep rock, which rises from a great domed base about 96 km (60 miles) across. Deep valleys run into this base and both the wildlife and the flora are extraordinary. Thick mountain forest covers the lower slopes, to a height of about 3,047 m (10,000 ft), and leopard, elephant, rhino and buffalo are among the animals that occasionally stray higher into the strange moorland that covers the middle

Pages 76 – 7: a climber sizes up one of the dizzying crags of Table Mountain with the city of Cape Town spread out beneath his feet. Table Mountain was first climbed in the spring of 1503 by the Portuguese Admiral Antonio da Saldanha, who wanted to check his bearings. Today it is the home of South African rock climbing and one of the most climbed mountains in the world with more than 500 recognized routes, most of them difficult rock climbs. The cliffs of the 1,087 m (3,566 ft) mountain have been weathered into a surface that makes it possible to climb in the most unpromising looking places.

Left: the snows of Kilimanjaro, Africa's highest mountain, sparkle in splendid isolation above the Masai savannah, only 320 km (200 miles) from the Equator. This dormant volcano is one of the largest in the world, rising to 5,895 m (19,340 ft) at Uhuru Peak. The main crater is 2·5 km (1·5 miles) across and still emits sulphurous fumes. A belt of high montane forest, inhabited by wildlife including elephant, buffalo and rhino, encircles the peak below 3,000 m (10,000 ft). Above the trees there is a belt of giant heather forest which eventually fades into a dry lava scree at about 4,000 m (13,000 ft), where there is little flora beyond the occasional helichrysum, giant groundsel and moss. Today the climb is very popular with tourists and there are some excellent ice and rock routes among the summit peaks for the more ambitious.

slopes. Here giant heather grows to a height of 6–9 m (20–30 ft). Above the heather, from about 3,505 m (11,500 ft) upwards, the moorland is dotted with bizarre giant plants; for example, a type of groundsel grows into 6 m (20 ft) trees, and lobelia grows to 1·5 m (5 ft).

Being only 17 km (10 miles) from the Equator, Mt Kenya enjoys a special climate. During August and September, when its northern flank is 'in condition' for climbing, the other side is swathed in snow and ice, while during the January-February dry season the southern side has summer weather.

The rock of the old volcanic plug forming the summit peaks is excellent for climbing, the combination of snow, ice and rock being similar to that found on the Central Alps in Europe. In recent years the potential for climbing on

the winter side of the peaks has been realized, and some very fine climbs have been made, on both rock and ice. The most impressive new routes have been on ice, particularly the 'Diamond Couloir' and 'Ice Window' climbs in the 500 m (1,500 ft) gullies of snow on the steep southwest face.

## Mount Kilimanjaro

The highest mountain in Africa at 5,895 m (19,340 ft), Kilimanjaro is a uniquely beautiful mountain of Himalayan scale. It provides climbs of extreme difficulty as well as relatively easy routes for the tourists, most of whom make it as far as the crater rim but do not attempt the final trek of just over a mile to the top of Uhuru Peak.

As on Mt Kenya, thick tree cover

blankets the base of the mountain below 3,000 m (10,000 ft), except where there are banana and coffee plantations, some of which reach as high as 1,800 m (6,000 ft). The heather forest above the trees is even wilder and more impressive than that of Mt Kenya. At about 4,000 m (13,000 ft) the heather gives way to dry lava scree, on which only mosses and the occasional giant groundsel and helichrysum grow.

The principal peaks on Kilimanjaro are Kibo, the crater rim, of which Uhuru peak is the highest part, and Mawenzi, some 12 km (7·5 miles) across the saddle. Mawenzi is another and older centre of volcanic activity rising to 5,148 m (16,890 ft). The third peak is Shira, 4,004 m (13,140 ft), which has nothing to offer the climber but is a beautiful moorland plateau.

The ordinary route up Kibo, known as the Marangu Route, is simple and there are huts for visitors who usually reach the crater in about four days. Altitude sickness takes a heavy toll of those who attempt the mountain. For climbers, the Kibo summit peaks and those of Mawenzi offer spectacular routes amid awe-inspiring scenery, and some of the climbs demand a high standard, such as the classic Heim and Kersten glacier routes on the south and southeast faces.

Circling the mountain at about 4,300 m (14,000 ft) makes an interesting four-day expedition, and in 1971 two climbers, Howell and Snyder, made a complete traverse of the Kibo and Mawenzi peaks, taking eight days.

## Ruwenzori

Since the dawn of recorded history, legend had it that the source of the River Nile was a snow-fed lake among high mountains deep in the heart of Africa. Geographers and travellers had handed on the story and it was Ptolemy of Alexandria, writing about AD 140, who labelled these mountains the 'Mountains of the Moon'. Nevertheless, the Europeans who were exploring Africa a hundred years ago found it difficult to believe that there could really be snow-covered peaks on the equator.

In 1876, the explorer Henry Stanley sighted 'an enormous blue mass' away in the far distance but it was not until 12 years later, on another expedition, that he realized the significance of this mass.

'While looking to the south-east and meditating upon the events of the last month, my eyes were attracted by a boy to a mountain, said to be covered with salt, and I saw a peculiar-shaped cloud of a most beautiful silver colour which assumed the proportions and appearance of a vast mountain covered with snow. Following its form downwards, I became struck with the deep blue-black colour of its base, and wondered if it portended another tornado; then, as the sight descended to the gap between the eastern and western plateaus, I became for the first time conscious that what I gazed upon was not the image or semblance of a vast mountain, but the solid substance of a real one, its summit covered with snow ... It now dawned upon me that this must be Ruwenzori.'

During the 1890s a number of expeditions gradually built up a picture of this strange group of mountains. It was not a single massif but a series of six major snow-draped peaks strung along a range nearly 130 km (80 miles) long and separated by huge gorges plummeting several thousand feet into the tropical rain forest.

Left: Mount Kenya, with its great ice-hung summit peaks standing only 16 km (10 miles) south of the Equator, is an amazing sight as it soars 3,658 m (12,000 ft) above the surrounding savannah of East Africa. The twin summits, seen here from the south-west in the Teliki Valley, are the eroded plug of a volcano that is estimated to have once topped 7,010 m (23,000 ft). Today Batian, *left*, stands at 5,199 m (17,085 ft) and Nelion, *right*, some 11 m (36 ft) lower. The Gate of Mists between the two peaks, with Diamond Glacier and Diamond Couloir below, contain the most spectacular new routes on the mountain. For aesthetic beauty and simplicity of line there is little in Africa to equal the

near-vertical ice climb up the 366 m (1,200 ft) Diamond Couloir. Because of objective dangers such as avalanches it was long considered suicidal, and climbers must take care to choose the right conditions.

Top: the Berber village of Around, close to Toubkal Massif in the High Atlas mountains of Morocco.

Above: the colourful VIP tent at a Berber festival in the Anti Atlas mountains of Morocco.

Top: giant groundsel or 'tree groundsel' are in flower on the slopes of Mt Kenya in January. This weird moorland, in which the humble groundsel grow into 6 m (20 ft) trees and the silky lobelia up to 1·5 m (5 ft), is separated from the thick mountain forest below 3,050 m (10,000 ft) by a zone of giant heather growing up to 9 m (30 ft) high.

Above: this giant lobelia at Lake Kitandara, 4,023 m (13,200 ft) in the Ruwenzori Range, is one of the many exotic plants found in these Ugandan 'Mountains of the Moon', one of the sources of the great Nile River.

Left: ice cliffs along the crater rim of Mt Kilimanjaro.

In 1906 the ubiquitous Duke of the Abruzzi arrived with a large party of impressive climbing ability, accompanied by scientists and naturalists. Mounting what was almost a Himalayan assault, with 150 porters hired to carry the equipment, the party set off to climb all the major peaks and to map the entire area.

After the Italian expedition had climbed more than a dozen of the highest peaks (including Mount Margherita which at 5,109 m (16,763 ft) is the highest peak of the Stanley group) and the surveyors and naturalists and photographers had done their work, Ruwenzori lost some of its mystery. But it was more than 25 years before another expedition was mounted.

The higher peaks are characterized by spectacular formations of ice-rime that build up into great cornices and mushroom shapes on rock and ridge. Down below, the slopes boast a particularly deep and slimy bog, several small dark lakes and, as with Mounts Kenya and Kilimanjaro, a spectacular flora of giant heather and groundsel, often draped with moss, which gives the approaches a moody atmosphere. The frontier of Uganda and Zaire cuts through the range.

## Southern Africa

The mountains of southern Africa stretch from the southern tip at Cape Town, with its famous Table Mountain, eastwards and then north as far as Natal. They do not form a single range, but a series of ranges.

Table Mountain, 1,087 m (3,566 ft) high, became the home of South African mountaineering, following the first meeting of the Mountain Club in 1891, and with almost 500 recognized routes on its sandstone faces, it is now one of the most climbed mountains in the world. Generally, the routes are difficult.

The major climbing area in Southern Africa lies west of Durban among the Drakensberg (Dragon) mountains, known to the Zulus as *Quathlamba*, or Barrier of Spears. These run for hundreds of miles along the rim of the high interior plateau, the highest mountains and the centre of sporting interest being on the border between Lesotho and Natal. An interesting feature of the caves in the area are splendid Bushman rock paintings, while outside there is plenty of wildlife, including baboon, eland and sometimes leopard. Curiously, the highest peak in southern Africa, a summit in Lesotho named Thabana Ntlenyana (The Little Black Mountain), 3,482 m (11,425 ft) high, was not discovered until 1951.

Almost all these mountains are now readily accessible by road. The popular areas for skiing in South Africa are in the mountains immediately north of Cape Town. There are centres at the Hex River Mountains, 140 km (85 miles) north-east of Cape Town, on Waaihoek, 1,951 m (6,400 ft) high, and Matroosberg, height 2,251 m (7,386 ft) and there is also some interest in winter snow and ice climbing in that area.

The African mountains have never been a Mecca for climbers as have the Himalayas, but the love of mountains is reserved not only for the biggest or most spectacular; it is concerned with the valleys as much as with the high peaks. Something of the spirit of this love was captured by the South African statesman and elder of the Commonwealth, General Jan Smuts, in a speech he delivered on Table Mountain in 1923:

'The mountain is not merely something eternally sublime. It has a great historic and spiritual meaning for us. It stands for us as the ladder of life. Nay, more; it is the ladder of the soul, and in a curious way the source of religion. From it came the Law, from it came the Gospel in the Sermon on the Mount. We may truly say that the highest religion is the religion of the Mountain. What is this religion . . . ?

'The religion of the mountain is in reality the religion of joy, of the release of the soul from the things that weigh it down and fill it with a sense of weariness, sorrow and defeat . . . Not only on the mountain summits of life, not only on the heights of success and achievement, but down in the valleys of drudgery, of anxiety and defeat, we must cultivate this great spirit of joyous freedom and uplift of the soul. We must practise the religion of the mountain down in the valleys also.'

# AUSTRALIA, NEW ZEALAND AND JAPAN

Australia has remarkably few mountains for such a large continent, the greater part of its area being flat and barren. In the centre stand the Macdonnell and Musgrave Ranges with the famous sandstone hump known as Ayers Rock. However, these mountains and hills are of little interest to climbers or skiers, and Australian mountain activity is concentrated in the southern part of the Great Dividing Range which follows the line of the eastern coast, from Cairns to Melbourne.

Here at the southern end of the range, between Sydney and Melbourne, stand the Snowy Mountains, with Mount Kosciusko at 2,230 m (7,316 ft) the highest point in the continent. There are no permanent snow fields here, but this area is the centre of

Previous pages: Mount Stirling, 160 km (100 miles) north-east of Melbourne in Victoria, stands at the southern end of the Great Dividing Range, close to the popular ski centre of Mount Buller, 1,807 m (5,928 ft). As skiing becomes ever more popular in Australia, the slopes of Mount Stirling and the surrounding peaks are being adorned with ski lifts and other facilities for the tourist.

Left and above: the Blue Mountains of New South Wales rise to a series of plateaux of about 1,066 m (3,500 ft), some 130 km (80 miles) from Sydney on Australia's eastern seaboard. They are composed of an elevated crust of red sandstone and shale, cut through with great timbered valleys. Ironstone staining tints cliffs and crags such as

Kanangra Walls, *left*, and 'Lion's Head', *right*, with hues of rust-red, tangerine, purple and brown. The valleys are floored with eucalyptus and the oil from these trees in the air intensifies blue light rays, for there is nothing blue about the mountains themselves. The colours are most spectacular towards sunset when dust particles in the air also enhance the red light rays. Rock climbing has been extensively developed in Australia since the 1950s, mainly on rocks near the big coastal cities of the south-east.

Facing page: Mount Cook in New Zealand's Southern Alps is the centre of antipodean mountaineering. Here it is seen in November from the Hooker Valley to the south. Rising to 3,764 m (12,349 ft), Mount Cook is one of the world's great mountains. The Southern Alps typically provide tough and dangerous mountaineering in which skill in snow and ice work is vital.

Left: the extraordinary whale back of Ayers Rock stands near the exact geographical centre of Australia. According to Aboriginal legend this 230-million-year-old sandstone rock is where the human race was fashioned, and there is evidence of primitive habitation in the area.

Australian skiing. Indeed, Australia has the longest unbroken history of skiing as a sport, the first ski club in the world being founded at the Kiandra mining settlement in 1861. The season begins on the Queen's birthday in June and is over by the end of September. Conditions are rather like those in Scotland, or New England, and the weather is changeable, with spring snow a fleeting pleasure and powder snow a rarity. For cross-country skiers there are some long, exciting routes that are almost in the nature of expeditions.

Tasmania is better endowed with good climbing mountains, although they are hard to reach because of thick bush and harsh weather. The rock faces around Mount Ossa, height 1,167 m (5,305 ft), and such summits as Federation Peak and Frenchman's Cap hold long climbs on excellent rock.

For the really determined, New Guinea has some magnificent mountain terrain and the third largest equatorial ice cap after those in East Africa and the Andes. The highest summit is Carstenz Pyramid, at 5,039 m (16,532 ft), and climbing on huge rock walls along this mountain spine is reported to be excellent by those enthusiasts who have coped with the near impenetrable jungle, tangled foothills and glaciers, and political hurdles.

## New Zealand

New Zealand's South Island is blessed with as fine a range of alpine mountains as anybody could wish for. The Southern Alps run the length of this beautiful island, fronting its western side and taking the full brunt of the prevailing north-west wind off the Tasman Sea. For this reason the weather is notoriously unreliable, and rainfall very high.

In Mount Cook, 3,764 m (12,349 ft)

high, and its surrounding peaks, New Zealanders have one of the great mountains of the world. The region has been a national park since 1953 and it is the heart of antipodean mountaineering.

The Maori name for Mount Cook is *Aorangi* (the Cloud Piercer). It stands at the centre of the Southern Alps. The range is more or less in the same latitude south as the European Alps are north. However the snow line is about 600 m (2,000 ft) lower, and the mountains provide tough, dangerous climbing in which snow and ice work is of paramount importance. It is not surprising that it is in this sort of terrain that New Zealand mountaineers excel, and indeed Ed Hillary practised on Mount Cook before tackling Everest.

In 1882 the Reverend William Green made a gallant attempt on Mount Cook, together with the alpine guides Emil Boss and Ulrich Kaufmann of Grindelwald. Several times they were pushed back. Finally, they found a route on the northeast side of the mountain and climbed to within 61 m (200 ft) of the summit before being turned back by nightfall.

'From the moment we had gained the arête, anxiety about beginning the descent had filled our minds,' Green wrote, 'as should darkness overtake us on the summit of the mountain, our chances of ever returning to the haunts of men would be but slight.'

The descent was worse than any of them had expected, and they spent the night standing on a narrow ledge desperately trying to keep awake until morning.

Following this brave effort, five more attempts were made between 1886 and 1890, but those too failed short of the summit.

Finally, on Christmas Day 1894, three New Zealanders made the ascent via the Hooker Glacier – a dangerous

route not repeated until the 100th ascent in 1955. The local men, Thomas C. Fyfe, George Graham and Jack Clarke, were inspired to make the attempt by the news that the wealthy amateur mountaineer and explorer Edward Fitzgerald had sailed from Europe, together with the guide Matthias Zurbriggen, intent on making the first ascent. Fitzgerald arrived in New Zealand only a week before the successful attempt by Fyfe's party, and he was bitterly disappointed. Despite this, he and Zurbriggen were able to make first ascents on five other major peaks, and Zurbriggen made the second ascent of Mount Cook – solo – by what is now the normal route, the Zurbriggen or northeast ridge.

These mountains provide a very high standard of climbing, and the huge 2,290 m (7,500 ft) Caroline face of Mount Cook, its southeast face, used to be held in the same kind of awe as the Eigerwand in Europe. This enormous ice wall was finally climbed in 1970, more easily than had been expected, creating a psychological as well as a technical breakthrough in New Zealand mountaineering.

Mount Tasman, one of the mountains first climbed by Fitzgerald, is thought by many people to be the most beautiful mountain in the Southern Alps. At the more southerly end of the range, the hazards of ice and rock climbing are compounded by the difficult access through dense forest and across wild rivers. Although the normal routes on Mount Cook and other peaks are fairly straightforward, the rock is often poor and the weather unpredictable, which makes any climbing here a serious business.

Skiing in New Zealand is really in the category of serious ski-mountaineering, except on the Ruapehu Ski Fields on North Island. There the mountains are actively volcanic

and provide open, moderately steep slopes. In South Island there are more than 17 ski fields, but access is usually difficult. The main activity here is ski-mountaineering and often airlifted glacier skiing.

## Japan

Japan's highest mountain, Mount Fuji, or Fujiyama or Fujisan, is one of the most famous and one of the most beautiful mountains in the world, a perfect volcano rising to 3,776 m (12,390 ft). Less well known to westerners are the Japanese Alps, which are comparable to the European Alps in beauty, and form the rugged backbone of the country.

The Japanese Alps are divided into three ranges, north, central and south, with 26 peaks of more than 3,000 m (9,843 ft), mostly composed of steep, sharp-ridged granite. In winter the snow cover can be deep, and with strong winds, high humidity and temperatures down to −20°C (−4°F), the mountains command respect.

Whereas in all the other countries mentioned so far, the love of mountains was largely the result of western influence, this is not true of Japan. It was not wholly true of China or India or the Himalayas either, for throughout the East, respect for mountains played an important part in traditional religion. They were not disliked, loathed, or ignored as they had been in the Middle Ages in Europe. However, the Japanese were more active in their reverence of mountains than other Eastern peoples.

For more than a thousand years, the Japanese had regarded their mountains, and particularly Fuji, with a mixture of reverence and aesthetic appreciation. Many mountain tops in Japan were crowned with a shrine or temple and the most active mountaineers at the start of the 19th century were members of the *Koju* sect who made annual ascents of their chosen sacred mountain carrying special octagonal staves and dressed in white robes.

Mountains also form an important part of Japanese art, and Mount Fuji, rising just 88 km (55 miles) from Tokyo, has always held a special significance for the Japanese in this context.

The idea that the summit of a moun-

Mt. Kosciusko is the highest peak in Australia, rising to 2,229 m (7,316 ft) in the Snowy Mountains at the southern end of the Great Dividing Range. The range is largely clothed in forest and is better suited to the trekker or 'bushwhacker' than the mountaineer, so that most climbing development has been on cliffs and rocky outcrops. There is skiing in the Snowy Mountains, although there are no permanent snowfields.

Left: the beautiful symmetrical cone of Mount Fuji, the highest mountain in Japan at 3,776 m (12,390 ft). There are Shinto shrines on the summits of many of Japan's mountain peaks, including Mount Fuji, and the importance of mountains in Japanese religious beliefs has made western-style mountaineering readily acceptable.

Above: the Japanese are enthusiastic skiers as well as climbers and trekkers, so much so that the slopes become crowded as some 10 million skiers a year take to the mountains.

tain is an excellent place for contemplation and spiritual rejuvenation was also held by some of the early European climbers. Perhaps significantly it was an English minister, the Reverend Walter Weston, who brought the western idea of climbing mountains as a challenging sport to Japan.

Since then Japanese mountaineering has developed along much the same lines as elsewhere, with increasingly difficult ascents at home, followed by new and harder climbs in Europe and expeditions to America, the Himalayas and other great mountain ranges. In the last three decades there has been an enormous increase in Japanese interest in mountains, particularly following the triumph of 1956 when a team climbed Manaslu in the Himalayas, the eighth highest peak in the world at 8,156 m (26,760 ft).

In overseas expeditions the Japanese outnumber any other nation, by a good margin, and they climb right at the frontiers of current expertise and technology, often going for the spectacular routes. In Europe they headed straight for the Eigerwand where their efforts were characterized by the extensive and expensive use of aid techniques: one party of five men and a woman in

1969 forced a second *diretissima* (straight up) route on the Eigerwand, using 250 bolts, 200 rock pitons and a mile and a half (2·4 km) of fixed rope. In the Himalayas, the Japanese were the first to attempt the south-west face of Everest in 1969, reckoned to be the hardest way up the world's highest mountain, while the first woman to climb Everest was a 35-year-old Japanese, Junko Tabei, who made the ascent in 1975.

And it is not only the Japanese climbers who have taken to the mountains, especially since the Second World War; skiing too has boomed in Japan, with an estimated 10 million skiers using the slopes each year. Half of these are reckoned to be beginners who have a try and then give it up, but even so the slopes in Japan are crowded. Skiing takes place predominantly on dormant or extinct volcanoes below 2,000 m (6,500 ft), and over ground that has a dense cover of vegetation. Sometimes this vegetation is an attraction, as at the resort of Zao in Yamagata which is famous for forests of low stunted pines that in winter become completely mummified in hoar frost and driven snow. These pigmy ice-figures are known as *chouoh* and are prominent in Japanese mountain art. There are some 400 ski centres, and the scenery in which they operate is often very beautiful. Access to these centres is generally easy by road, and perhaps this is one reason for the popularity of the sport. Powder snow is rare and spring snow is a transitory pleasure.

Skiing and climbing are of course not the only ways in which the Japanese enjoy their mountains. Trekking is popular too. Also, despite the changes of the 20th century in Japan, the contemplative view of mountains remains a major factor in contemporary Japanese culture.

# GLOSSARY

**Abseil** – or 'rappel' – to slide down a rope using friction to control the descent.

**A cheval** – to climb a narrow ridge with a leg on either side of it.

**Aid climbing** – also known as 'artificial climbing' – the use of specialized gadgets to make progress on ground that could not otherwise be climbed.

**Aiguille** – French for needle, used to mean a sharply pointed rock peak.

**Alpenstock** – long wooden pole tipped with a ferrule, now superseded by the ice-axe.

**Alpine style** – to tackle a mountain as quickly and lightly as possible, as opposed to 'Himalayan style' where equipment is set up in a series of camps up to a peak.

**Arête** – sharp ridge of ice or rock.

**Belay** – technique used by climbers to safeguard each other from a fall by attaching themselves and their rope to a rock; a spike of rock so used.

**Bolt** – expanding bolt screwed tightly into a previously drilled hole in a rock face.

**Chockstone** – see Nut.

**Col** – dip in a ridge, usually between two peaks.

**Cornice** – curl of snow or ice overhanging the edge of a ridge or plateau, and formed by the wind. Cornices can be quite big and look solid, so they are always dangerous, especially in poor visibility.

**Couloir** – gully on a large mountain.

**Crampon** – steel frame fitted to climbing boots with 12 points on each foot to grip on ice.

**Free climbing** – see Aid climbing – climbing without using artificial aids to make progress. On ice it means using only ice-axe, crampons and hammer, and not pitons, except to provide protection.

**Ice-axe** – essential piece of equipment for snow and ice work. Consists of a hardened steel head shaped into an adze on one side and a spike on the other. The end of the handle is also tipped with a steel point.

**Karabiner** – or Krab for short – a snap link with a spring-loaded gate used for all kinds of attachments.

**Nut** – metal or plastic chock which can be wedged in a crack to give protection. The use of these instead of pitons has greatly changed modern free climbing. A chockstone is a stone jammed in a crack for the same purpose.

**Piton** – steel peg or spike driven into a crack in rock or ice to support climber or rope.

**Running belay** – or runner – a form of protection where the rope is run through a Krab on a sling attached to the rock or ice by a piton or nut, so the distance a climber may fall is limited to the length of rope between himself and the last 'runner'.

**Sérac** – ice cliff.

**Sling** – loop of tape or rope, used especially in running belays.

**Three-point contact** – to move only one hand or foot at a time so that the climber always has three holds.

**Traverse** – horizontal section of climbing; also a route over a mountain from side to side, or over more than one peak.

**Verglas** – thin ice covering on rock.

Left: Mt Tasman, 3,498 m (11,465 ft), is a most impressive-looking peak in New Zealand's Southern Alps. Seen here from the east, the Silberhorn is to the left of the ice-clad summit, with the classic Silberhorn Ridge falling precipitously to the ice fall of the Hochstetter Glacier. Even the easier route on the narrow South West arête over the Silberhorn is pretty difficult, and the Balfour or West Face holds one of the most challenging of hard modern face climbs.

# INDEX

# ACKNOWLEDGMENTS

The publishers would like to thank the following individuals and organizations for their kind permission to reproduce the photographs in this book, and Dr. C. R. A. Clarke and John Cleare for their valuable help.

Adespoton Film Services: 61 below right; Ardea London: (P. Morris) 15 above, (Jean-Paul Ferrero) 16 below, (K. W. Fink) 40 below, 41 above and below, (Su Gooders) 67 below, (Richard Waller) 68 above; Stephen J. Benson: 58 above, 86; Heather Angel/Biofotos: 90–91; Simon Brown: 44 above and below, 45; H. Adams Carter: 60–61; Norm Clasen: 49; John Cleare/Mountain Camera: 12–13, 17, 18–19, 21–24, 26–29, 50, 62–63, 65, 66, 71, 73 below, 80, 83 above and below; Bruce Colman Ltd: (Chris Bonington) Title Page, 7, (Eric Crichton) 15 below, (Pekka Helo) 16 above, (Jonathan Wright) 40 above, (Jen and Des Bartlett) 54–55, (Chris Bonington) 58 below, 70, 74, (Kim Taylor) 81 below, (V. Serventy) 89; Ed Cooper Photo: Contents, 6, 34–35, 36–37, 42, 48, 51; Gerald S. Cubitt: 82; The Daily Telegraph Colour Library: (Dave Waterman) 20; C. M. Dixon: 14, 32, 33, 81 above; Henry Edmundson: 72; Laurie Engel:

92–93; Derek Fordham/Arctic Camera: 52; The John Hillelson Agency Ltd: (Ian Berry) 76–77; Anthony and Alyson Huxley: 16 centre; Japan National Tourist Organization: 93 right; Terence McNally: Endpapers; William March: 39, 53; Marion and Tony Morrison: 56–57, 61 above right; Mountain Camera: (William March) 43; Natural Science Photos: (I. Bennett) 78–79; Captain J. Noel: 64 above and below; Janusz Onyszkiewicz: 67 above; Galen A. Rowell: 38, 46–47, 94; Spectrum Colour Library: 30–31, 84–85, 87; John Tyson: Half Title, 25, 68 below, 69, 73 above and centre, 75; Zefa Picture Library (UK) Ltd: (F. Breig) 10.11; Günter Ziesler: 59

Octopus Books is grateful to the following publishers for their permission to reproduce quotations from their publications:

Page 12—Sidgwick and Jackson: Sir Gavin de Beer, *Early Travellers in the Alps*, 1930.
Page 15—Oxford University Press: T. Graham Brown and Sir Gavin de Beer, *The First Ascent of Mont Blanc*, 1957.
Page 22—John Murray: E. Whymper, *Scrambles Amongst the Alps During the Years 1860–1869*, 1871.
Page 24—Eyre and Spottiswoode: G. W. Young, *Mountains with a Difference*, 1951; Rupert Hart-Davis, London: Heinrich Harrer, *The White Spider*, 1959.
Page 30—Methuen, London: G. W. Young, *Collected Poems*, 1936.
Page 38—Yale University Press: William H. Brewer, *Up and Down California in 1860–64*, 1930.
Pages 38 and 41—Sampson, Low, Marston, Low and Searle, New York: Clarence King, *Mountaineering in the Sierra Nevada*, 1872.
Page 56–7—George Allen and Unwin: *The Autobiography of Bertrand Russell, 1872–1914*, 1967.
Pages 70 and 83—Newnes, London: Hugh Merrick, *The Perpetual Hills*, 1964.
Page 70—Edward Arnold, London: Eric Newby, *Great Ascents*, 1922.
Page 73—Edward Arnold, London: E. F. Norton, *The Fight for Everest 1924*, 1925.
Page 74—Hodder and Stoughton: Herman Buhl, *Nanga Parbat Pilgrimage*, 1956.
Page 75—Hodder and Stoughton: John Hunt, *The Ascent of Everest*, 1953.